reACTING

LAMDA

reACTING

A Fresh Approach to Key Practitioners

**by David Shirley, Penny Cherns
& Stephen Unwin**

PUBLISHED BY
OBERON BOOKS
FOR THE LONDON ACADEMY OF
MUSIC AND DRAMATIC ART

First published in 2007 for LAMDA Ltd.
by Oberon Books Ltd.
521 Caledonian Road, London N7 9RH

Tel: 020 7607 3637/Fax: 020 7607 3629

info@oberonbooks.com
www.oberonbooks.com

ISBN: 1 84002 755 X / 978-1-84002-755-6

Cover design: Joe Ewart for Society

Printed in Great Britain by Antony Rowe Ltd, Chippenham.

Contents

Author Biographies

DAVID SHIRLEY

Currently the Head of the BA (Hons) Acting programme in the School of Theatre at Manchester Metropolitan University, David trained as an actor at the Arts Educational Schools and spent many years working in theatre, film, radio and TV. Alongside an impressive career as a practitioner, David has taught extensively both in the UK and the USA. Specialist interests include actor/director training, Stanislavski, Shakespeare and his contemporaries and the Theatre of Samuel Beckett.

PENNY CHERNS

Penny trained on the Directors' Course at the Drama Centre and worked as Joan Littlewood's assistant before continuing as a freelance director in major provincial repertory theatres directing classics, modern plays and musicals. She was Associate Director at Chester, Watford and Nottingham Playhouse and worked at the RSC, the Royal Court and the New End theatres. She has also directed dramas for the BBC and Channel 4. She has taught international workshops worldwide and has taught and directed in the USA at Brandeis, Juilliard, Yale and the University of Iowa. In the UK she has taught at RADA, Drama Centre and Guildhall and is currently teaching at LAMDA.

STEPHEN UNWIN

Stephen Unwin is founding director of the English Touring Theatre for whom he has directed more than 20 productions of both classics and new plays. Before that he was Associate Director at the Traverse Theatre in Edinburgh and was responsible for a number of International and Scottish Premieres. He has also directed opera and theatre at the Royal Opera House, the National Theatre and throughout the world. His writing includes three pocket guides for Faber and Faber, *So You Want to be a Theatre Director* for Nick Hern Books and *A Guide to the Plays of Bertolt Brecht* for Methuen.

Introduction

This is a good book for anyone who wants to know more about how the modern trained actor operates. It is compulsory reading for anyone contemplating training to become one: the three subjects of the book are used by all of the major drama schools in the UK.

Every art form spawns theorists. Of the three, Brecht is the only playwright, the only artist – Stanislavski and Laban were, as it were, handmaidens to the art.

What actors have to do convincingly is pretend to be people other than themselves, inhabiting an imagined world. Properly ordered and executed, this becomes the art of theatre capable of producing the profoundest insights into our world and lives.

These theorists are concerned with *how* the actors pretend to be other people and what to do to achieve it. Two of the former, Stanislavski and Brecht, have an eye to producing acting for particular kinds of theatre.

Stanislavski was Chekhov's director and Chekhov's work pulled Russian theatre away from its contemporary operatic style of performance towards the style we now know as naturalism. Naturalistic acting remains the prominent style on our stages and screens to this day.

Brecht was concerned to provide actors for the kind of plays he was writing. These involved a technique of alienation which involves actors in not only inhabiting an imaginary character, but also in maintaining a presence in the performance of themselves as actors.

Only Laban had no particular theatrical axe to grind. His methodology for actors applied to any style of theatre.

None of the three invented so much as observed the actors' process and annotated what they saw, producing, finally, a comprehensive methodology: a journey in stages towards perfect performance, profoundly conceived and truthfully executed. On the one hand, acting without tricks and on the other, making the trick of acting so persuasive as to cause total belief in an audience – rather than requiring the suspension of disbelief.

All three methods, their terminologies, exercises and examples are in current use in acting training and none are more familiar with them than the three commentators who contribute to this book.

Peter James
Principal, LAMDA

Chapter One

Stanislavski's System: The Anatomy of an Actor's Art

by

David Shirley

Introduction

Born in Russia in 1863 to a wealthy manufacturing family, Konstantin Sergeevich Alekseev enjoyed what must surely have been a highly privileged and extremely stimulating childhood. Keen to encourage a taste for the arts in their children, Konstantin's parents regularly accompanied them on visits to the theatre, opera and ballet. Small wonder then, that at the age of only 14, Konstantin began producing his own plays in the fully-equipped theatre that his father had built on the family estate. Together with his eight siblings, Konstantin – or Kostya as he would have been known – experimented with and adapted mini-dramas and plays that were later staged for the entertainment of his parents and their guests.

From these early teenage investigations and youthful incursions, Kostya, who would later adopt the name of Stanislavski in his professional life, was to develop a lifelong passion for performance. A passion that would not only fuel his development as an outstanding and much acclaimed actor and director, but also help to foster both the emergence of a new kind of theatre and an alternative, often radical approach to actor training.

The influence of the 'System', as it has become known, is difficult to underestimate. From its initial inception at the Moscow Arts Theatre in 1906, where a group of irritated actors were forced to tolerate what appeared to be a series of 'eccentric' exercises, Stanislavski's 'grammar' of acting has established itself as a dominant feature of Western theatrical discourse. The first serious attempt to articulate a series of logical and coherent principles specifically related to the numerous impulses that inform the actor's creative process, the System laid the foundations for an entirely new approach to actor training. When, in the years following the emergence of the Soviet Union in 1917, the Moscow Arts Theatre – under Stanislavski's leadership – toured Europe and the

United States, the company's fame spread. Indeed, such was the acclaim and fascination with the group's work that many of its most gifted practitioners sought new lives outside of Russia as actors, directors and teachers. This factor, coupled with the increasing availability of English and European translations of Stanislavski's own writings, helped further his ideas on acting and subsequently promoted the efficacy of the System in the West.

Although much of what Stanislavski's System advocates may now appear obvious, it is important to bear in mind the kind of background against which it emerged. During the latter half of the 19th Century, the Imperial theatres of Moscow and St. Petersburg favoured 'low-risk', popular forms of entertainment that ensured wide appeal and maximum income. Strict censorship meant that morally challenging or politically subversive material was prohibited. Instead, audiences were offered highly conventional forms of melodrama and vaudeville featuring formulaic character types such as the lover, the low-life and the villain. Actors were expected to adopt particular archetypes and embody the physical gestures and vocal mannerisms with which they were associated. Established custom meant that audiences could expect to see favourite actors recreate familiar roles in new plays. In this tradition, the play came a poor second to the personality of the 'star' actor and the idea of an ensemble was unheard of. With no training to speak of and alarmingly short rehearsal periods the quality of performance was generally regarded as poor. Stanislavski's intense dislike for such forms of theatre is evidenced in the first of his three famous books on acting. Warning against the pitfalls of depending on superficiality, the enigmatic Tortsov – Stanislavski's surrogate acting tutor – counsels his students as follows:

'With the aid of his face, mimicry, voice and gestures, the mechanical actor offers the public nothing but the

dead mask of non-existent feeling. For this there has been worked out a large assortment of picturesque effects which pretend to portray all sorts of feelings through external means.' (1)

An Actor Prepares by Konstantin Stanislavski

It was in his efforts to reject such pretence and formulate a richer, psychologically complex and emotionally more demanding system of performance that Stanislavski was to devote much of his working life.

Always a prolific writer, Stanislavski maintained a lifelong habit of transcribing his thoughts on theatre and acting. As a consequence, it is possible to glimpse the origins of the System in some of his earliest notebooks, a number of which were completed when he was just 14 years old. How, for instance, might it be possible to judge the quality of one's own acting? When is a performance truthful? Is it possible for an actor to reveal the psychological dimensions of a role? In later years, the answers to these and numerous other questions pertaining to the actor's craft would find an outlet in some of the various publications that bear Stanislavski's name. Through his own work as an amateur, later a professional actor and subsequently as one of the founding directors of the Moscow Arts Theatre, Stanislavski experimented with and perfected the techniques that would have a profound influence on the development of realist performance practice in both theatre and film.

Towards the end of his life, Stanislavski had amassed a vast array of journals, lesson plans, notes and book drafts. By the time of his death in August 1938, he had approved the publication of two major works: the autobiographical *My Life in Art* (1924) and the first of three famous acting manuals *An Actor Prepares* (1936). The latter was initially intended to form part of a much larger volume entitled *An Actor's Work on Himself.* Due to what was felt to be its excessive length, however, Stanislavski agreed to divide the work into two halves, the second of which was published posthumously in 1949 under the title *Building a Character*. The final volume, *Creating a Role*, which is a compilation of various draft manuscripts and production notes, was published in 1961, 23 years after his death.

Whilst, at one level, the effort to record his ideas on acting and develop them into a formal system for training is certainly theoretical in scope, it is important to recognise the great efforts that Stanislavski took in order to ensure that his ideas retained their essentially practical and organic relevance. Rather than simply offer endless descriptions of tried-and-tested techniques or provide us with a list of instructions, Stanislavski organises his material in such a way as to arouse curiosity and provoke reflection. Through the creation of a fictional classroom in which imaginary students attempt to master key exercises and grasp new ideas, Stanislavski explores both the mysteries of acting and the nature of theatre art. Just as we begin to comprehend one concept, Tortsov confronts us with the complexities surrounding another. The result is that the reader, like the students that attend the classes, becomes utterly absorbed by the intricate range of problems that are presented. As with any acting class, there are confident and not-so-confident students, introverts and show-offs, sceptics and devotees. Through detailed analysis, practical illustration, argument, discussion and rehearsal, Stanislavski gradually puts forward a complex, but extremely dynamic set of principles which, when taken together, constitute a remarkably coherent and consistent practical guide to an actor's craft. Far from reaching a point of closure or completion in his work, Stanislavski continued to refine existing ideas and experiment with new ones until the end of his life. Indeed, at the time of his death, he was in the midst of delivering a series of new classes to a hand-picked group of eager students at the Opera-Dramatic Studio, based in his own apartment in Moscow. It is imperative, therefore, to view his work as a lively and progressive series of experiments and investigations into the uniquely challenging, often illusive and occasionally profound modes of communication that the theatre makes available.

What follows is an attempt to offer a clear insight into the workings of the System and the various elements contained within it. Key components and concepts will be discussed in detail and, wherever possible, a series of practical exercises and questions will accompany each section. The overriding aim is to encourage both intellectual understanding and practical competence in this multi-faceted, highly dynamic and impressively holistic approach to acting.

The Art of Acting

In the second chapter of *An Actor Prepares*, Stanislavski identifies five different modes of acting: *living the role, representing the role, the mechanical reproduction of the role, overacting* and *exploitation*. Of these, only the first is considered suitable for the kind of artistic approach to which Stanislavski aspires. If a performance is to realise the fullest artistic potential then it is necessary for the actor to appreciate the importance of the need to 'live the part'. In other words, the actor is required to take account not just of the physical life of the character, but also the inner life:

> *'He must fit his own qualities to the life of this other person, and pour into it all of his own soul. The fundamental aim of our art is the creation of this inner life of a human spirit, and its expression in an artistic form'*(2)

> *An Actor Prepares* by Konstantin Stanislavski

If the theatre spectator is to gain any real insights into the nature of humanity, then it is imperative that actors begin to look and sound like real human beings. For this, it is necessary for the performer to take account of the psychological aspects of a role and determine the extent to which inner impulses can become manifest in outer behaviour. At the root of Stanislavski's art is the assumption that the more convincing an actor's performance – the more realistic it appears – then the more likely it is to provoke a reflective and emotive response from the spectator. The ability of human beings to empathise with each other, to mutually experience pain, grief, joy and so on, represents one of the key principles informing much of Stanislavski's work. Whilst there is no doubt that Stanislavski emphasises the need for his actors to look and sound like real people, he is acutely aware that many of the fictional situations they are likely to encounter will appear entirely alien. How are actors to portray complex situations in which the characters experience thoughts and emotions that are not their own? How can they begin to make the carefully rehearsed – the artificial – appear lifelike and spontaneous, as if it were happening for the first time? For Stanislavski, it is in the attempt to make those watching an actor's performance believe in its spontaneity and empathise with the character's experiences that the art of acting begins. Thoughts and emotions are considered essential components in the construction of credible characters and it is only when his students have begun to understand the importance of this aspect of human nature that the principles informing Tortsov's training regime can really begin to take effect.

The other modes of acting described in the chapter – though not all without merit – fall considerably short of the creative insight that Stanislavski demands. Whilst the *representational* style of acting certainly attempts to re-create the emotional life of the character, it does so only inasmuch as it allows for an impression of an emotion rather than the emotion itself. Whilst actors of this kind might certainly dazzle us with their brilliance, delicate and intricate human feelings are likely to be glossed over, resulting in a performance technique that *'is less profound than beautiful'*(3).

Whereas *representational* acting at least attempts to reference genuine human feeling, *mechanical* modes of performance avoid it completely. Instead performers rely on a series of hackneyed conventions that are designed to replace any sense of genuine emotion. Though more or less extinct now, such performance techniques were widely used in the melodramas and vaudevilles that enjoyed enormous popularity in the 19th Century. Established clichés such as the hand on the heart as an expression of love, rolling the eyes as an indication of jealousy or the use of exaggeratedly high or low vocal tones in moments of joy and despair are common examples. Through its dependence on a series a highly stereotypical external conventions, acting of this kind is entirely devoid of anything even resembling an inner life and consequently was ill-suited to the artistic techniques Stanislavski set out to develop.

The remaining examples referenced in the chapter are not so much formal acting styles than instances of undisciplined and unfocused performance practice. The first, which is referred to as *overacting*, results from a poor attention to detail and gross generalisation. It involves little thought or preparation and is built entirely on external traits and mannerisms. Finally, we are offered an example of what is described as *exploitation* in which, instead of serving the demands of the material or the interests of the company, individual performers use acting as a means of exhibiting what they consider to be superior qualities such as beauty, personality and charm. Performers of this kind are the *'deadliest enemies of art…and if they cannot be reformed must be removed from the boards.'*(4)

Although each of these examples of performance practice is analysed and discussed separately, Stanislavski emphasises the point that it is only from a theoretical perspective that the work of an actor can be divided into such categories. In practice all actors, even the most accomplished, experience moments – sometimes in a single performance – when the potential for true artistic insight is marred by the tendency to resort to convention or rely on the ability to charm and seduce the audience.

For acting to be taken seriously as an art form, Stanislavski believed that it was necessary to avoid the need to rely on personality, stereotype or mimicry and work instead to develop the habit of 'living the role'. Once this has been achieved even the smallest, seemingly insignificant details become part of a rich interpretative landscape which the actor can use to begin to fine-tune a performance and convey the minutiae of human behaviour and social interaction.

Relaxation, Focus and Concentration

Relaxation

In order to begin to work creatively, it is necessary, first of all, for the actor to reach a state of relaxation in which the body is free of unwanted tension and the muscles are loose and flexible. To convincingly embody both the inner and outer life of a character, the performer needs to develop a sensitive and expressive body that is alive to the nuances and vicissitudes of dramatic circumstance and situation. Muscular tension and physical unease inhibit the actor's ability to work freely. It is essential, therefore, to develop strategies that will ensure maximum physical release and openness.

The need for physical training is at the very heart of Stanislavski's methodology. *'You cannot at the very beginning of our work, have any conception of the evil that results from muscular spasms and physical contraction'*(5). Although not the subject of in-depth analysis and discussion, the physical aspects of the work undertaken by the students that feature in *An Actor Prepares* are clearly important. All students attend regular classes in gymnastics, dancing, fencing and singing – the chief aim of which is to develop, train and fine-tune a controlled and expressive use of the body.

Due to the very public nature of their work – often on vast stages, in front of large audiences, under the glare of powerful lighting etc. – actors are predisposed to extreme forms of tension and, as a consequence, the often detailed and moving work that is undertaken in rehearsal can be severely undermined. It is well known that fear can often have a paralysing effect which locks the body and produces an entirely fixed, almost rigid appearance. The dilemma facing the actor is that of finding a way of dealing with the natural fear and nervousness that accompanies performance, whilst at the same time maintaining a state of complete physical relaxation.

Stanislavski's solution to this problem is to encourage the actor to develop an enhanced degree of self-awareness. Through a series of repeated and systematic exercises, the actor will develop a capacity for internal observation that will prove invaluable in controlling and eliminating unwanted tension and stress. Such a process must be developed to the extent that, even in the most dramatically exciting or challenging moments of a performance, the instinct to remain relaxed is stronger than the tendency to allow the body to become tense. In order to achieve such a perfected state of relaxation, Stanislavski insists that the 'inner observer/controller' of our muscles must become an innate part of an actor's physical make-up. Such a condition can only be realised when the habit of relaxing muscles is developed *'daily, constantly, systematically'* so that it proceeds *'while we are going to bed or getting up, dining, walking, working, resting, in moments of joy and of sorrow'*(6). Only through the subconscious management and elimination of physical tension and stress will the actor prevent it from interfering with the instinct to be creative.

In order to begin the process of removing physical tension, it is first of all necessary to become conscious of it. The following exercises are designed to promote a stronger sense of physical awareness and lay the foundations for establishing the internal observation and control that Stanislavski's System demands.

Exercises Promoting Physical Awareness

- Lie in a semi-supine position on a smooth, flat surface (eg the floor of the classroom) with the knees raised so that the soles of the feet, which should be slightly apart, are in full contact with the floor. Try to ensure that the full length of the spinal column is also in contact with the flat surface. Starting first with the toes and gradually moving up through the body to the ankles, calf muscles, knees, pelvis, chest, arms, shoulders, neck, face and head, contract each group of muscles as tightly as you can for a count of ten before releasing them and resuming as full a state of relaxation as possible. This exercise should be done slowly and carefully and close attention paid to the difference between muscles that are tense and those that are relaxed. Try to isolate each group of muscles so that only specific areas of the body are tense at any one time.

- Go through exactly the same process, only this time instead of lying on the floor, walk slowly around a good sized room and examine the effects of muscular tension in different parts of the body.

Try to develop a sense of how tension in the ankles, knees, pelvis, back etc. affects the rest of the body. Having completed the process with as many groups of muscles as possible, continue walking around the room with a relaxed and fluid physical demeanour. Where there is tension try to eliminate it so that the body moves as freely and openly as possible.

- Adopt a physical position that involves either crouching on the floor or stretching outwards and upwards and try to locate and release areas of tension. Using your imagination to make sense of different positions will prove enormously beneficial in this exercise. For instance, when crouching try to imagine that you are crawling through a very small, cramped place or when stretching, imagine reaching to catch a ball that has been thrown just out of your reach.

So that you can begin to monitor and check your growing self-awareness, it is useful to begin working with a partner who can identify areas of tension in your body that may have gone unnoticed. Using the above exercises, verify with your partner whether or not your muscles really are tense/relaxed/free.

Having completed this stage of the work, the next step is to begin to foster the development of an instinctive ability to identify and remove unwanted physical tension. By promoting increased self-reliance and enhanced physical control, the next group of exercises enable the establishment of the internal controlling impulse that Stanislavski describes.

Exercises Promoting Increased Physical Control

- Lift a reasonably heavy object – such as a toolbox, a suitcase or a small table – and, without moving, hold it for a few moments. Take the time to identify those areas of the body where there is tension. Apart from the group of muscles that are being used for the task of lifting and holding the object, every other part of the body should be relaxed. Check that this is the case. Repeat the exercise a second time, only instead of actually lifting the object, *pretend* to do so. Mime lifting the toolbox, suitcase or table etc. Once again check the physicality for areas of tension. Ideally, the same group of muscles used for lifting the first time around will have contracted again. If not, can you make them contract? Remember to check that those areas of the body not involved in the mimed lifting are relaxed and free.

- Repeat the above process, only this time instead of maintaining a fixed position, begin to move around the space. Once again, find a real reason to be lifting and moving the object, an imagined circumstance of some kind – taking it to a different part of the room, carrying it for a friend etc. As in the case of the first exercise, take the time to scan the body to eliminate unwanted areas of tension. The task is slightly more difficult this time because of the action involved. Nevertheless, don't allow unnecessary tension to creep into the body merely because you are moving. When you are satisfied that only those muscles necessary for performing the task of lifting and moving the object are engaged, go through the process again, only this time perform the actual movement involved, but mime the object you are carrying. Where is the tension? It should be the same as when you were actually carrying the object. Try to eliminate unwanted physical stress and ensure that only the required muscles are contracted.

- Standing in a relaxed position with the feet slightly apart, isolate and move different areas of the body.

Lift the upper part of the right leg, for instance, so that the knee is at a 90 degree angle to the torso and hold that position for one minute. Turn the head and neck muscles to the left and hold that position for one minute. In each case, check to ensure that tension is kept to an absolute minimum and that only those muscles that are actually needed for each movement are engaged. Finally, try folding and unfolding the upper body downwards and upwards from the waist checking the extent to which you can isolate the individual joints that make up the vertebrae column. There are actually 24 in total from the base of the spine to the top of the neck. How many can you pick out?

- During the course of a given day, whilst washing and dressing, on the way to college or work, queuing for lunch in the canteen, reading, watching TV, in the bath or lying in bed, take a few moments to scan the body for areas of tension. Quickly identify and isolate which muscles are actually needed for the task you are undertaking. Where tension occurs in muscles that are not actually in use try to relax and free them.

In order to reach the level of internal awareness that Stanislavski's System requires, it is important to be able to identify the difference between wanted and unwanted tension. Not all forms of tension are destructive. Without the innate capacity to tense and release muscles at will, it would be impossible to undertake even the simplest of actions like walking, lifting or carrying. For this reason it is important to ensure that in each of the physical exercises undertaken there is a balance between moments of tension and release. Only then can the actor begin the process of learning to recognise which forms of muscular tension are necessary and which are not.

Equally important is the need to understand that because a muscle is relaxed it does not mean that it should be slouched. In an ideal state, muscles that are relaxed should also be ready to respond immediately to demands that we place on them. Sluggish or tired muscles are inefficient and do not perform well under stress.

Focus and Concentration

Learning to focus and concentrate in such a way as to become immune to the tendency to be distracted by anything that is extraneous to the world of the play is of the utmost importance to Stanislavski's way of working.

To illustrate the point, *An Actor Prepares* includes an episode in which Torstov relates a Hindu tale of a Maharajah, who, in a quest to find the most suitable candidate to undertake the role of minister, announces that the position will be given to the person that can carry a dish filled to the brim with milk around the top of the city walls without spilling a single drop. After many failed attempts, a man came forward who – despite taunts and abuse from the crowd, threats and gunshots from the army, false fire alarms and terrifying screams – succeeded in completing the task. When asked why he was not distracted by the surrounding commotion, the newly elected minister declared that he heard and saw nothing and that his attention was solely concerned with the need to avoid spilling the milk.

If one considers the artificial environment of a stage space where, in the presence of often large and not always sympathetic audiences, actors are required to reproduce considerable amounts of memorised text, cope with physical tension and nervousness, deal with technical effects such as sound and lighting and handle props that are often far removed from the objects they actually represent, the potential for constant distraction and loss of focus is huge.

When one of his students confronts him with a similar observation, however, Tortsov, with his customary frankness, responds as follows:

> *'You feel powerless in the face of such a task… and yet any simple juggler in a circus would have no hesitation in handling far more complicated things, risking his life as he does it'* (7)

An Actor Prepares by Konstantin Stanislavski

To begin to overcome the various forms of distraction that an actor is prone to, it is necessary to channel and control concentration in such a way as to ensure that the focus of attention is always directed at the creation of the imagined world of the play rather than the real environment of the theatre/performance space. Needless to say, the imagination, something to which we will return later, has an important role to play here, but without an understanding of how to develop concentration and focus attention in such a way as to release the imaginative impulse, any connection to the imagined world of the play can only ever be tenuous.

In order to start to develop the ability to concentrate on stage, Stanislavski suggests that it is necessary to find a way of dealing with and managing the actor's awareness of the audience. To help eliminate the risk of becoming overly conscious of the *'black hole'* (8) that represents the auditorium, Stanislavski recommends constructing an invisible wall between the stage space and that of the audience. By directing the actor's attention behind the footlights instead of in front of them, both the instinct to 'show off' as well as the tendency to become overly self-conscious is considerably reduced. As one becomes more accustomed to the use of such a technique it is possible either to place imaginary objects on the 'fourth wall', eg a clock, a mirror or a painting, or to extend its boundaries so that the wall becomes a marker for a distant horizon. The important thing is to ensure that direct eye contact with the audience, either in general or with particular individuals, is completely avoided. Instead, actors must work towards the achievement of what Stanislavski referred to as a state of *'solitude in public'*(9) in which concentration and focus are developed to such a degree that instead of experiencing feelings of nervousness and anxiety, the actor begins to tune into the various elements that make up the imagined world of the play – objects, spaces, characters, relationships and so on.

At this point, it is important to note that although Stanislavski's approach certainly aims to reduce the actor's preoccupation with the spectator, there is no attempt to suggest that the performer should ignore the audience entirely. To force or insist on the pretence that one is actually alone is contrary to the *shared* and very *public* nature of theatre art. The notion of achieving a state of 'public solitude' necessarily involves an acknowledgement of the audience's presence and as such embodies an artistic technique that is designed to foster a heightened state of concentration.

Having established the principle of the 'fourth wall', Stanislavski goes on to describe three different levels of concentration that are appropriate to the work of the actor. These 'circles of attention', as they are described, offer the means of engaging the imagination and concentration at a level that is appropriate to the needs of particular kinds of dramatic situation.

The first circle of attention encompasses a small, clearly-defined area, in which the actor is the centre and which may also include a few small objects on a table, for instance, or a nearby desk. By focussing attention on the objects included in this space, which might initially be defined by the use of light, and learning to observe detail in a relaxed and unforced manner the actor can begin to experience what is perhaps the strongest and most sustained sense of 'public solitude'.

The next circle of attention involves using a larger area that includes an increased number of objects, some items of furniture and possibly some people as well. Once again, the actor is placed at the centre of the circle and this time concentration and focus are extended to take account of every detail of the larger space. Rather than attempt to achieve a 'generalised' state of concentration, it is important for the actor to examine small sections of the area in detail before moving on to embrace the circle as a whole.

Finally, there is the third, and most demanding circle of concentration, which might initially include everything on stage, but can be extended to include the full auditorium as well – to imply a distant horizon, for instance, or a small vessel on a vast ocean.

Movement between these circles of attention can often prove difficult in that the larger the circle the more likely it is that concentration and focus will dissipate. To circumvent this problem, Stanislavski recommends reducing the size of the circle to that of the first and concentrating on smaller objects before gradually increasing the size of the circle.

By continuing to practice this technique so that the actor becomes comfortable with moving between and adapting to different levels of concentration, the ability to focus at exactly the level that is required by the dramatic moment will be greatly increased. Moreover, the ever-present threat of distraction will be kept in abeyance.

Alongside the ability to develop attention in relation to external phenomena, Stanislavski also emphasises the need to develop internal attention, by which he means *'the things we see, hear, touch and feel in imaginary circumstances'* (10). *'The objects of your "inner attention"'*, he asserts, *'are scattered through the range of your five senses'*(11). For Stanislavski, the acting process requires the performer to draw on both material (external) and abstract (internal) sensations. In either case the qualities pertaining to such sensations – size, shape etc. – can be real or imagined and it is necessary for the actor to become adept at moving between the two. In the case of internal attention, there is an added complication in that imaginary objects – due to the mind's tendency to wander – demand an even more disciplined use of focus and concentration than real ones. As in the case of learning to focus and concentrate on the external environment, however, the mind too can be disciplined and trained in such a way as to develop the skill of inner focus.

The following groups of activities and exercises are designed to help develop increased powers of observation, focus and inner concentration:

Exercises to Develop External Focus and Concentration

- Ask a friend to fill a tray with a collection of small items eg a ball of string, a teaspoon, an egg cup. Spend a few moments looking at the objects and then remove the tray and try to remember the contents. As you become more skilled at this exercise, begin to increase the level of description for each item so as to include colour, texture and size. Start with observing about 20 objects over a three minute period at first and gradually increase the number to about 30 or 40 whilst simultaneously reducing the amount of time available for observation. The aim of this exercise is to observe and register as much detail as possible. It is important, therefore, to handle and inspect the objects closely and compare the way in which you describe them to that in which they actually appear.

- Ask a friend to arrange 20 different items – eg pencils, books, photographs – on a table or a desk. Spend two minutes observing the arrangement before turning away and asking the friend to remove everything. Now replace each item in accordance with exactly the same arrangement as you first observed them.

- Using a blindfold, taste different kinds of food. Can you describe the difference between red grapes and white grapes, between a watermelon and a honeydew melon, between a Gala apple and a Granny Smith, between red and white cabbage, between white, plain and dark chocolate?

- Repeat the same exercise only this time instead of tasting foods see if you can identify substances according to their scent eg foodstuffs, fragrances, flowers, detergents, alcohol.

- Ask a friend to wrap up an item that is unfamiliar to you and of an unusual shape, weight and texture. Using a blindfold, unwrap the item and describe the way it feels. Is it rough or smooth, heavy or light, blunt or sharp?

- Try to identify different sounds that are taking place close to you, but out of sight eg drawing, washing a floor, folding paper.

Exercises for the Development of Different Levels of Concentration

- Sit at a table in a large, preferably unfamiliar, room and define three circles of concentration; small, medium and large. Observe and digest the contents of each circle taking in as much detail as possible – colours, shading, texture and weight. Begin to get a sense of how things appear from a distance as well as close up. After about 15 minutes leave the room and describe it in as much detail as possible to a colleague. Return to the room with the colleague and compare your description to the observations of your colleague. What details were missing? How accurate was your description?

- Spend no more than one minute observing a friend that is beside you. Look at the colours and texture of the clothing, the physical features and stance, the possessions that they have around them. Turn away and describe what you have observed to a third party who continues to look at your friend. Compare your description to what the third party sees. How accurate are you?

- Repeat the same exercise only this time observe a person that is further away from you – say within the scope of a second or third circle of attention.

- Spend a few moments listening to the sounds that are in your immediate environment – the kitchen, for example, or your bedroom. Enlarge the focus of attention so as to include the sounds that are in the rest of the home. Extend the range further so as to include the noise from the street immediately outside your home. Describe in detail the sounds that take place in each zone of attention. It is often useful to do this exercise with a friend and compare notes afterwards.

Exercises for the Development of Internal Focus and Concentration

- Last thing at night before going to sleep, spend some time recalling the events of the day. Focus on one activity in particular eg a particular train journey, a lecture, a pleasing meal. Try to recall all the sensory experiences afforded by the event in as much detail as possible. Visualise and recall all of the sights, sounds, smells, tastes and feelings involved. For the first few evenings start with small events such as an evening meal, before gradually building up to more detailed recollections, eg a party or a trip to the seaside.

- Recall a multi-sensory event that took place at some point in the not too distant past – a special Christmas, for instance, or an exciting birthday party – something that remains fairly vivid in your memory. Begin to flesh out the details of the event in your mind – what made the event enjoyable or special, what colours, sounds, tastes, aromas can you recall?

- Bring to mind a good friend or family member and see if you can build up a strong mental image of this person in an environment that is familiar to both of you. How is s/he dressed? What particular features stand out? What position are they in? What is his or her mood and tone of voice? How vivid a mental impression can you make of your chosen person and the surrounding environment?

Central to the process of developing the ability to concentrate and focus is the need to closely observe the world around us. If an important aspect of an actor's work is to recreate human behaviour and experience, then it is vital to develop the habit of watching and studying the environment in which we live. How human beings respond and relate to each other in moments of joy, conflict, anxiety and stress etc and the ways in which our physical mannerisms, facial gestures and speech can provide an indication of how we feel internally, offers an important platform on which to build creatively meaningful and artistically rewarding portraits of humanity.

Imagination

It is in the attempt to observe and make creative and artistic use of the events and things that we see around us that the actor's imagination comes into play. *'There is no such thing as actuality on stage'*(12), Stanislavski advises us in the fourth chapter of *An Actor Prepares*. Instead, the actor must develop the ability to transform the fictive world of the play into a *'theatrical reality'*(13). The most important element in this transformative process is the imagination. It is vital, therefore, to ensure that this aspect of an actor's technique is highly cultivated and extremely agile. If the imagination is unable to personalise and own the dramatic events represented in the play, how can an actor even begin to engage the imagination of the spectator?

For Stanislavski, imagination also includes the realm of fantasy. Unlike the imagined, however, which is based on the possibility that something can be or could happen, fantasy involves the invention of things that have no material existence or which will never take place. For him, both imagination and fantasy are inextricably linked. To highlight this idea, Stanislavski reminds us that whilst the flying carpet is a product of fantasy, aviation or space travel certainly is not. For the dedicated actor it is every bit as important to invest credibility and a sense of truth into a portrayal of the Cowardly Lion that features in Frank Baum's *Wizard of Oz* as it is for the role of Hamlet in Shakespeare's famous play. Both characters feel isolated, both are capable of great warmth, both have great potential and both lack courage. Each character, of course, is fictitious, but whilst one is very clearly the product of fantasy, the other can quite easily be imagined.

In order to arrive at a creatively satisfying and artistically truthful interpretation of a given role, it is necessary for an actor to pay very close attention to what might at first strike us as insignificant detail. What has happened to the character before the play begins, for instance, or between the scenes in which the character appears? To what extent might outward behaviour confirm or contradict the character's inner feelings? How can the various relationships presented in the play help to shape our understanding of the character's personality? To what degree can the actual lines be used in such a way as to indicate psychological complexity and subtle shifts in temperament or mood?

If an actor is to begin working on a role in this way, then it is important to be able to steer the imagination so as to ensure that it serves our interpretative needs. It is first necessary to retain a strong sense of logic and coherence in the things we try to imagine. Even in moments of fantasy, it is important to ensure that it is possible that one set of given circumstances can arise from another. *'Always remain in close contact with logic and coherence'*, Tortsov urges his students, otherwise the imagination will *'balk at being asked to work from a doubtful premise to a stupid conclusion'* (14).

Equally important is the need to avoid vagueness or generality and work instead to flesh out the specific details of each character, relationship or given set of circumstances.

> *'Suppose you take a journey around the world. You must not think it out "somehow", or "in general", or "approximately", because all those terms do not*

belong in art. You must do it with all the details proper to such a large undertaking'(15)

An Actor Prepares by Konstantin Stanislavski

Moreover, if we can link all of these 'details' into a chain of imagined circumstances that are accompanied by a corresponding series of inner visions, every moment of the play will be illustrated for us in such a way as to stimulate a character's changes in mood or emotional shifts. To make the point clearer, Stanislavski uses the metaphor of film and suggests that the action of the play must become like a moving picture that plays itself out on the screen of the actor's inner vision. It is through this process of internalising the content of the play that the actor begins to personalise the events it depicts.

Whilst such a technique might at first appear rather complicated, the starting point is remarkably straightforward. By recourse to what he refers to as the *'magic if'*(16), Stanislavski points the way to a technique that makes it possible for the imagination to begin to justify almost any given set of circumstances. What if it were a sunny, warm day today instead of a cold, dark one? How would my behaviour change? What if it was night instead of day? What if it was the last day of term instead of the first day? What if I was born 20 or 30 or 40 years earlier? How might my view of the world shift?

By ensuring that all creative investigations are justified by suppositions of this kind, it becomes possible for the imagination to test out a whole range of interpretative ideas. Even simple things like chairs and tables can move from functioning as thrones and altars to castles, ships and pyramids.

Closely related to the notion of the *'magic if'*, is the idea of what Stanislavski refers to as the *'given circumstances'*, which describes all the details of the play and the actual style of the production, including the dramatic narrative, the period in which it is set, the location, the events depicted, the design concept, the director's aims and the actor's interpretation. Close attention to this level of detail helps to focus the imagination and enable the actor to make specific and appropriate interpretative choices that are informed by the context in which the play is staged. If the *'magic if'* provides an essential starting point for the imagination, then the *'given circumstances'* help to ensure its continued development.

> *'"If" gives the push to the dormant imagination, whereas the "given circumstances", build the basis for "if" itself. And they both, together and separately, help to create an inner stimulus'* (17)

An Actor Prepares by Konstantin Stanislavski

When the imagination is stimulated to the stage where it becomes possible to establish a truthful and credible connection to the fictional world and life of the character, then it is more likely, Stanislavski suggests, that the actor will be able to convey real emotion and true feeling. Importantly, Stanislavski distinguishes between pursuing an emotion for its own sake and focusing on the *'given circumstances'*. Whereas the largely subconscious nature of emotions makes them difficult to command, the *'given circumstances'*, by means of research and careful observation, are easily accessible. Once an actor has a firm grasp of these and knows how to use them in such a way as to influence a character's outward *behaviour*, Stanislavski believes that the emotional responses will follow quite naturally without the need to force them. For this reason Stanislavski places great emphasis on the need for careful definition in relation to every aspect of the *'given circumstances'*. By advocating the use of the *'magic if'* as a means with which to engage the imagination and the *'given circumstances'* as a way of nourishing it, Stanislavski believes that it will become entirely possible for the actor to convey a sense of complete transformation both in relation to his/her own physical and inner life as well as that of the surrounding environment.

To help initiate the process of understanding and personalising the play in such a way as to begin to bring about this kind of transformation, Stanislavski recommends organising our thoughts in such a way as to undertake careful reflection on the following six questions – the answers to which can only be found from several extremely close readings of the play and in-depth research into the period and culture in which it is set:

Who am I?	This question relates to the character's age, background, education, influences, likes, dislikes, relationships, habits and personality traits.
When is it?	Is it winter, spring, summer or autumn? What is the year, the month, the time of day?
Where am I?	What is the place that I am in? What surrounds me – furniture, objects, textures and colours? Is this my own environment or does it belong to somebody else?
What do I want?	The answer to this question helps to locate the character's need, desire, or intention. What previous events have brought me to this point?
Why do I want it?	This provides the justification for the thing that the character needs or desires. Such a justification must be strong enough to fuel all of my actions.

How will I get it? What future actions must I undertake in order to achieve the thing that I want? What must I do?

Of these six questions – *Who?*, *When?*, *Where?*, *What?*, *Why?* and *How?*, Stanislavski urges us to pay particularly close attention to the fifth – *Why?* In attempting to find an answer to this question, the actor is forced to clarify the character's thoughts and make *practical* sense of his or her actions. The emphasis on the need to reach a practical understanding of the character's actions is important, since for Stanislavski, a collection of abstract facts or intellectual concepts is of little value. Rather than use the above questions to embark on an intelligence-gathering exercise, the aim is to find ways of connecting all of the discoveries that are made in the imagination which, for the actor, must always be evidenced through action.

Inevitably, the imagination will be more developed in some people than in others and, as a consequence, some actors find it easy to empathise with the fictional lives of dramatic characters. Whatever the individual case, Stanislavski was keen to point out that the imagination, like a physical muscle, can be developed and trained. The following exercises are designed to begin this developmental process and stimulate imaginative responses to material objects as well as ideas:

- Using a painting or an old photograph of someone that is entirely unknown to you, begin to outline an imaginary biography of the person depicted. Examine the picture very closely so as to reach decisions about age, tastes, habits etc. Where was this person born? What did s/he do for a living? Rather than simply guess at the answers to these questions try to piece together the answers by studying the details contained in the picture – the background against which the subject is standing, for instance, often provides important clues! Look at the facial expression, the posture, the hands and feet and the way in which the person is dressed. Having completed this task, give the portrait to a partner and ask them to go through the same process. Compare notes.

- Working in a small group use the *'what if'* technique to transform the appearance and texture of everyday objects. A screwed up piece of paper, for instance, can become a mouse with a broken leg, a screwdriver can become an ice lolly or a potato a human heart. Try to ensure that in each case the focus is directed at imparting to the actual object the qualities of the imaginary one. Avoid playing out personal responses to what is imagined – it is the object itself rather than what you feel about it that is important.

- Explore the extent to which the use of the *'what if'* technique can change your relationship to different objects. How might your relationship to a particular book, for instance, change if it was a) a long overdue library book, b) recently bequeathed to you by a deceased grandparent, c) an illegal copy of a book that has been banned by the authorities, d) a book that you have saved for a long time to buy.

- Recall a recent event in your private life – a party, a holiday, a wedding etc. Starting with small details begin to imagine how things might have been different under changed circumstances. If it were night instead of day, for instance, summer instead of winter, or if certain key participants were missing. How might your own behaviour as well as that of other people have changed? Gradually increase the degree of change so that the event becomes less real than a fantasy. Try to retain a sense of logic and coherence and, wherever possible, find justifications for the adjustments that are made.

- Using a character from a favourite play as your subject, provide detailed answers to all of the six questions given previously. Ensure that each answer is as informative as possible and that it includes information that stimulates your imagination. In order to undertake this task it will be necessary to read the chosen play quite a few times and undertake some research into the period in which it is set.

As has been previously stated, not everyone possesses a vibrant and active imagination. If a performer, however, is to fully realise the artistic potential afforded by the theatre and enable the spectator to share in the many forms of fictional experience that it makes available, it is essential to pay very careful attention to this aspect of an actor's craft.

A Sense of Truth

One of the great paradoxes of Stanislavski's System is that, whilst it recognises the fictional and highly constructed nature of theatre art, it is predicated on the insistence that everything becomes real in the imagination of the actor. Unlike actuality, imagined truth is based on a series of presumptions and suppositions which become available to us through use of the *'magic if'* and the *'given circumstances'*. Unless the actor can find a way of believing in the character's situation and the world of the play, the performance will lack credibility. In this kind of theatre, it is the actor's ability to make the audience believe in the people and events depicted, that forms the basis for theatrical truth.

At this point it is important to recognise that, for Stanislavski, the notion of 'theatrical truth' is made up of two separate, but closely interwoven elements – *truth* and *belief.* For Stanislavski, *truth* in the theatre represents *'scenic truth'*(18), which is realised when the actor has succeeded in personalising the character, the given circumstances and all of the actions that are pertinent to the play. Once this has been achieved it becomes possible for both the actor and the audience to *believe* in the reality of the internal feelings and sensations that are represented on the stage.

> *'Truth on the stage is whatever we can believe in with sincerity, whether in ourselves or in our colleagues. Truth cannot be separated from "belief", nor "belief" from truth. They cannot exist without each other and without both of them it is impossible to live your part, or to create anything'*(19)

An Actor Prepares by Konstantin Stanislavski

Conversely, Stanislavski reminds us of the need to recognise and maintain an awareness of the fact that theatre is a form of artifice, which requires the audience to suspend disbelief and invest in the imaginative possibilities it affords. The extent to which an audience is willing to 'conspire' in the creation of a fictional world is entirely dependent on the actor's ability to appear credible and convincing. A sense of what constitutes an *untruthful* or *false* moment of interpretation, therefore, will prove invaluable in helping the actor decide at precisely what level to pitch a given performance – thereby reducing the tendency to overact or indeed to become fixated by certain seemingly 'dramatic' moments at the expense of others.

For Stanislavski, the theatre is at its most effective when it provides us with truthful glimpses into the workings of the human spirit and it is only when this level of representation is achieved that acting can truly be described as an art form. Whilst a depiction of the material environment in which the drama is situated certainly helps to prompt our imaginative processes, ultimately they are of no value beyond providing a framework in which to contemplate and reflect on the human condition. It is not the objects in and of themselves – the furniture, props, costumes, sets etc. – that make an audience believe in the dramatic circumstances, but the quality, nature and scale of the human involvement. If all the other aspects of a production are entirely detailed and realistic, but the actor's portrayal of a given role lacks a sufficient degree of truth and credibility, the performance is destined to prove a failure.

Although Stanislavski encourages the actor to reveal the psychological or 'internal' dimensions of human experience, he is only too aware that such an enterprise is only possible when very close attention is paid to the importance of physical or 'external' behaviour. For him, there is no inner impulse that does not find expression in physical action of some kind – an avoidance of eye contact, perhaps a sigh, or even a moment of complete stillness. Rather than approach a role by attempting to stir and reproduce the emotional life of the character, the System emphasises the need to identify a series of physical actions that can be used to lay the foundations for recreating a meaningful and truthful emotional response to each dramatic situation. The choice of which actions to perform must be justified by the given circumstances, the character's aims and the action of the scene. Each movement or gesture must be sufficiently detailed so as to arouse a strong sense of belief and conviction in the performer. Only when there is a consistent interplay between physical and psychological behaviour is it possible to stimulate the psycho-physical approach that Stanislavski advocates. Whilst it is certainly most important for an actor to have a clear intellectual grasp of a character's inner life – hidden feelings, desires, emotional responses etc. – the most practical way of accessing such experiences is through a clearly defined and carefully selected process of physical actions. The *Method of Physical Actions*, as this approach has become known, provides the most reliable means of ensuring that all forms of emotional expression are spontaneous and organically connected to the dramatic situation that the actor is trying to convey.

To illustrate the effectiveness of this approach *An Actor Prepares* (20) includes a sequence in which Tortsov invites one of his students to mime a series of actions leading up to a particularly tragic moment in a carefully selected improvisation. By insisting, in the first instance, that the actor mimes the scenic action, paying very close attention to even the smallest, seemingly imperceptible physical details, the tutor enables the student to identify a detailed *score* on which to base the physical action of the scene. For the student, the results prove something of a revelation:

> 'The moment I was convinced of the truth of my physical actions, I felt perfectly at ease on the stage.' (21)

> *An Actor Prepares* by Konstantin Stanislavski

In addition to promoting a greater sense of relaxation and ease on the stage, this approach also encouraged the actor to adopt a much more improvisational and organic connection to the work. By ensuring that all of his actions were highly detailed and carefully justified, the student was able to experience greater spontaneity and artistic freedom and as a result the performance appeared much more truthful and 'lifelike'.

With careful analysis, extensive improvisation, and continuous repetition, it is possible to build up a complete score of actions for a given role. By developing a coherent and logical chain of activities in this way, the actor can arrive at a much more informed *practical* understanding of the play and the thoughts and ideas it sets out to convey. Moreover, by promoting an enhanced degree of awareness of the ways in which the physicality acts as an indicator of a character's mental or emotional state, the actor can begin to develop a much more sensitive and expressive use of gesture.

By setting out to consciously justify and create the physical aspects of a given role, Stanislavski maintains that the actor will succeed in stimulating a chain of corresponding subconscious responses. What makes this approach particularly appealing is the way in which it combines intellectual, imaginative, intuitive and physical processes into a cohesive whole.

Closely related to the *Method of Physical Actions* is the idea of *Emotion Memory*, a technique which helps to further motivate and arouse internal feelings and emotions. Essentially, this approach involves a process whereby the actor draws from feelings that have resulted from personal experience and transfers them to the life of the play. Rather than retain emotional experiences in their original detail, Stanislavski maintains that our memory scatters them through our subconscious so that only a series of remnants and partial impressions remain. With the progression of time, the most vivid of these provide a kind of synthesised memory of once significant and sometimes even painful events.

'Time is a splendid filter for our remembered feelings – besides it is a great artist. It not only purifies, it also transmutes even painfully realistic memories into poetry' (22)

An Actor Prepares by Konstantin Stanislavski

For the actor, this store of *emotion memories* provides an invaluable reference point that can help to clarify and fine tune the represented feelings of the character.

Whilst this process may certainly involve a high degree of empathy and personal investment on the part of the performer, it is important to stress that it is designed to foster feelings in the actor that are analogous to those of the character rather than replace them entirely. Any attempt to re-create one's own emotional experiences on stage instead of those of the character – which emerge from a specific set of given circumstances, at a particular time and place – amounts to an unnecessary form of indulgence. It is most important, therefore, to make a clear intellectual and physical distinction between learning to draw from personal experience in order to motivate and shape feelings and emotional states that are akin to those of the character, and colonising and replacing such feelings with those of your own.

To begin to be able to work truthfully and with a genuine sense of integrity it is most important to pay very close attention to even the smallest details of each dramatic moment. The following exercises are designed to illustrate the importance of such detail and enable the actor to begin to lay the foundations for future rehearsal/performance practice.

- Using seven or eight consecutive minutes from your own immediate past life as the basis for a constructed 'scene', carefully recreate a series of recently performed activities involving physical action of some kind. This exercise works best when the chosen actions are selected from your daily routine – eg getting ready for bed, laying a table, tidying a messy room, packing for a holiday. Wherever possible the chosen scene should take place in the same location as that in which the actual events themselves occurred. Pay attention to the order in which events occur, to physical mannerisms, facial expression. Try to recall the thoughts and feelings you were experiencing at the time when these events actually took place. How spontaneously can you reproduce them? Repeat the sequence of events several times until you become familiar with them. Having completed this stage divide the activity into a series of much smaller actions that should be matched to corresponding inner thought feelings. Repeat each section slowly and carefully at first, before building up the speed to real time. Move through each section in this way until the entire sequence is formed into a *score of physical actions*. When you are satisfied that this is detailed and complete, run the entire sequence again. How accurately have you managed to recreate a realistic sense of the chosen actions? To what extent did your 'scene' feel alive and spontaneous? How far did the sequence of physical actions serve to stimulate inner feelings and thoughts?

- Choose a small extract or scene from a favourite play involving a character that you would like to portray. The extract should be no longer than three or four minutes in duration and should not involve moments of extreme physical action – no murders, suicides or battles etc. Having read the whole play several times and made careful decisions in relation to the biographical detail of the character and the given circumstances of the chosen sequence, begin to mark out a series of physical actions and gestures that you feel begin to evoke what happens in the scene. Such gestures should serve to reveal both the external activity of the scene (ie the physical things that the character actually does) as well as the internal impulses that inform or are prompted by them (ie the things that the character may be feeling). Ignore the dialogue of the scene at first and use only mimed gestures. The aim is to recreate a vivid and coherent sequence of actions that can later be used as the basis on which to build the content of the scene. When this has been achieved, slowly and carefully introduce the dialogue, paying particular attention both to the words themselves and the ways in which your *score of actions* might influence the way in which they are said – how they are communicated. Once this stage has been completed begin to introduce objects and furniture into the scene so as to begin to create a sense of the 'world' in which the action takes place. How do the details of this world – colours, textures, sounds etc. – influence your mood, temperament or feelings? Are such feelings analogous to those of the character? If not, what external details can you introduce to the scene in order to bring the feelings you are experiencing to those of the character? When you fully understand what internal feelings the character is experiencing begin to consider whether or not there have been episodes in your own life when you have felt something similar. If so, try to translate these feelings into the life of the character. Run the scene again allowing your own emotional energy to make contact with that of the character. Remember, the aim is to shape and craft the character's emotional responses not replace them with your own. Use your own experience, therefore, in the way an artist uses paint – as a means of creating something new. The colours already exist, but the image is entirely original. Due to the detail involved in this exercise, it is perhaps best to work on a scene involving an exchange between two characters. This means that ideas about the scene can be discussed and improvised and the work of finding props etc. can be shared.

- Once the above exercise has been completed go through exactly the same process with a different extract, only this time increase the level of dramatic tension and emotional energy.

Whilst the above exercises may appear painstaking in their attention to detail, it is most important to recognise that – as is the case with every other art form – the most moving and inspiring moments that occur in the theatre do not happen as a result of accident or casual generalisation. If an actor is to have any real success in revealing the highly complex, intricate and often baffling facets of human nature, then it is essential to recognise the need to develop a craft that is capable of absorbing and reflecting even the smallest and seemingly insignificant details that accompany every aspect of human behaviour.

Creating Relationships

Having explored the importance of learning to work in a relaxed, focused, imaginative and truthful way, it is now time to turn our attention to the need to create credible and appropriate relationships on stage. For Stanislavski, a stage relationship only becomes meaningful when the actors involved in a given scene have mastered the ability to communicate effectively. As with other aspects of the System, the aim here is to reveal the inner workings of the psyche, but unlike some of the techniques described earlier in the chapter, the emphasis on this facet of an actor's work is on the need to change and be changed by the objects and people that are around us.

> '...without absorbing from others or giving of yourself to others there can be no intercourse on the stage. To give or to receive from an object something, even briefly, constitutes a moment of spiritual intercourse.' (23)

> *An Actor Prepares* by Konstantin Stanislavski

Whereas in reality communication is based on an entirely spontaneous exchange of verbal and non-verbal signs and signals, many of which are involuntary, the contrived nature of theatre art imparts an added significance to the entire communicative process. It is as if the various processes by which we communicate are placed under a microscope and the audience is invited to look through the lens. Hence, Stanislavski's assertion that '...*if communication between persons is important in real life, it is ten times more so on the stage.*'(24).

In the theatre, of course, one of the primary means of communication is through the spoken word. In an essentially literary and aural medium, spoken language remains the most dominant mode of interaction. No less important for the actor, however, are the various forms of non-verbal communication. These range from physical gestures and facial expressions to variations in the tone, volume and speed of individual utterances. Often communication of this kind can highlight inconsistencies between the things a character is saying and the things s/he might be thinking or feeling. Through the use of non-verbal communication, or *subtext* as it is known, the actor can find ways of augmenting the meanings that are available in the playwright's words.

Stanislavski identifies two plains on which communication in a play takes place. The first involves direct communication between the actors during the course of dramatic action and the second functions indirectly with the audience who interpret such action and infer meanings from the ways in which it is presented to them. In some instances, it is possible for an actor to have direct contact with the audience – as with some of Brecht's plays, for example, or in the case of pantomime – but such approaches tend to undermine the seamless and unified forms of characterisation that Stanislavski's System favours.

To create genuinely convincing relationships on stage, it is necessary to establish a truthful and spontaneous flow of interaction between yourself and the other performers. Rather than try to build a relationship with imaginary characters or persons, it is important to enter into communication with the real people that are on the stage with you. They embody the 'world' of the play and are the means by which you can both produce and reflect changes in the given circumstances. Through a continuous 'unbroken' exchange of words, thoughts, gestures and feelings it becomes possible not only for the actor to personalise the experiences of the character, but also to share such experiences, indirectly, with the spectator:

> *'When the spectator is present during…an emotional and intellectual change, he is like a witness to a conversation. He has a silent part in their exchange of feelings, and is excited by their experiences. But the spectators in the theatre can understand and indirectly participate in what goes on on the stage only while this intercourse continues among the actors.'* (25)

An Actor Prepares by Konstantin Stanislavski

Once an actor is both intellectually and physically engaged in all of the processes by which real communication takes place – listening, absorbing, imagining, thinking, reflecting, embodying, speaking – it becomes possible to shape credible and appropriate stage relationships. Needless to say, in embarking on this aspect of rehearsal, it is essential to ensure that the kind of relationship that emerges is closely informed by and pertinent to both the given circumstances of the scene, the demands of the story and the personalities of the characters involved.

Rather than simply wait for a cue and then recite and direct dialogue at other performers, it is vital that an actor learns to interpret meanings behind words, gestures, tone etc. as well as to absorb and reflect the effects of such details in the physical behaviour of the character. Concentration observation, sensitivity and reciprocity, therefore, are of the utmost importance. No less essential is the need to ensure that every moment of communication on stage is organic and live. Rather than mechanically reproduce what has happened in rehearsal or in previous performances, it is imperative to establish new and 'unbroken' lines of communication for each moment of interaction.

Occasionally, an actor is called upon to communicate with an imaginary object or being – as in the case of Shakespeare's Hamlet when he is confronted by the ghost of his dead father (*Hamlet*: Act I, Sc. 5) or Macbeth, when the figure of the murdered Banquo appears before him (*Macbeth*: Act III, Sc. 4). At such moments it is important to make a distinction between the drive to make both the actor and the audience believe in the tangibility of the ghost and the need to convey an impression of the effects of such a vision on the *behaviour* of the character. In other words, it is the change that occurs in the character's behaviour that should be the focus of the actor's energy rather than the creation of an external imaginary presence. The use of the *'magic if'* will prove invaluable at such moments. 'What would I do if the unhappy and tortured spirit of someone I once loved appeared before me and spoke directly to me?'

Unlike previous exercises, the following tasks are designed to be undertaken with a minimum of one partner. If actors are to develop the skill of being able to communicate and respond truthfully moment by moment, it is absolutely essential to avoid the temptation to work alone. Ideally, the following exercises should be observed by a colleague, for instance, or a tutor – who can offer feedback and advice on the results produced. Whatever the case, it is very important to discuss each exercise very carefully before and after undertaking it.

- Ask a friend to relate to you the details of a meaningful event that has taken place in his/her life in the fairly recent past. The event should not involve a painful memory or anything that is of an overly personal nature, but it should be of significance. An important interview or audition, perhaps, an episode involving a confrontation of some kind, a tense visit to a hospital or the much dreaded arrival of a letter containing important exam results. Your partner should not play a character or do anything that is forced or superficial. Instead they should simply and clearly relate the details of the chosen event without overtly commenting on it. That is to say that wherever possible phrases such as 'I felt like this' or 'I was really frightened by that' should be avoided. During the course of your colleague's description of the event carefully observe the alterations that occur in his/her physical demeanour. What changes take place in the body, the face, the expression of the eyes? How does the tone, speed and volume of the voice change? Try to make a comparison between the actual words that are used and the speaker's mental (inner) attitude. What discoveries can be made about a) the speaker's public and private feelings b) the nature of the event itself and c) the impact it has had on the person to whom the event happened? When this exercise is completed in front of a group of people it can be revealing to have two or three 'observers' who then compare notes.

- Set up an improvisation involving two participants who are not allowed to speak. Let us say that they are both foreigners who do not share each other's language and have never met. Each has been instructed to meet the other in a public space – a park, a station or a bank – and to exchange important documents. They both know that they are under surveillance, so it is important to ensure that the documents are handed over to the right person. Gesture should be used sparingly in this exercise so as not to draw too much attention to a potentially dangerous and highly exposing set of given circumstances. How do the individual actors begin a process of communication and in what ways do they begin to test each other out? How does communication change from the beginning to the end – when they are unsure of each other to when they feel confident that the right person has been identified?

- Without the use of spoken language and in the presence of a partner, an individual actor should embark on a fairly complex imaginary physical activity – making a toy model, for instance, or sticking holiday pictures in a photograph album. The activity should be executed with absolute focus and total clarity. When the partner has fully understood the action that is taking place, s/he should join in the activity and help to complete the task. Once the partner has become part of this exercise it should be sustained for as long as possible in order to observe the silent communicative process that takes place between both participants. How do they interact with each other? How do we know when agreement has been reached or when one participant is confused?

- Set up an improvisation involving three people that have never met or spoken before. Possibly in a hospital when it is late at night and dark and all of the patients are tired. One of the patients has an operation the following morning and is rather nervous. Another is hoping to be discharged the following day and the third has just been admitted for observation. The participants shouldn't enter the improvisation with any specific aims or objectives that are extraneous to the situation described above. Instead each participant should listen and respond to the other two in such a way as to establish believable and meaningful relationships. It is the quality of communication that is important rather than the need to create a fictitious character. This exercise works particularly well in a shaded/dark room where the features of each actor can only just be made out. How easy or difficult is it to establish a continuous 'unbroken' line of communication?

- Working as a pair, set up an improvisation in which a conversation takes place between participants in different spaces. Where one person is downstairs and one is upstairs, for instance, or where one person is in the bathroom and the other is in a bedroom. The topic of conversation should not be overly intense, but it shouldn't be trivial either. The actual details need to be carefully discussed and agreed beforehand. It might prove revealing, for example, to discuss whether or not to go to a party – one person is really keen and the other would rather give it a miss. Alternatively, the discussion might be centred on the possibility of moving to a different part of the country – one of the participants has been offered a new job and is very excited, but the other is very anxious and not at all convinced that it is a good idea. Tune into your partner's tone of voice, vocal quality and pauses. How easy is it to interpret your partner's mood and feelings from the things that are said? At what points did your partner sound anxious, angry, disillusioned?

- Using the same or similar scenarios, repeat the exercise as above only on this occasion try to conceal your real feelings about the situation from your partner. Your feelings about the topic of conversation shouldn't change, but you don't particularly want to draw attention to them and you certainly don't want your partner to gain easy access to your actual thoughts. How does this exercise compare to the previous one? What observations can be made about the physical and vocal life of each scene? What adjustments need to be made when attempting to conceal one's feelings from those around us?

- Repeat both of the above exercises but instead of being located in separate spaces, imagine that both of you are in the same room. Let your use of gesture, eye contact (or the lack of it), facial expression, pause and vocal tone reflect meaning and reveal inner thought processes. How does the improvisation change when you can see each other? How much more difficult is it to hide one's real feelings or to endorse those of your partner? How easy is it to interpret your partner's feelings? In what ways do the feelings of your partner become physically manifest?

In order to become skilled communicators, it is important for actors to develop each of their five senses in such a way as to become alert to and tune into every aspect of human communication. With clear objectives, a well defined inner life and the ability to sustain focus and concentration, a performer can *'grasp'*(26) each vibrant moment of the play and in so doing seize and captivate the attention of the spectator.

Units, Objectives and Adaptations

In order to begin working on a play, it is first of all necessary for an actor to ensure that every aspect of it is fully understood. What is the narrative of the drama trying to convey to us? Why do the characters behave in the way that they do? What causes conflict in the play and how is it resolved? In what ways do unforeseen circumstances shape the actions of the characters? How does individual behaviour influence the experiences of the community? Without being able to offer accurate and detailed answers to these and other questions about the play, any interpretative work that is undertaken is destined to be the product of generalised and often highly inaccurate speculation. To begin to do justice to some of the complex situations presented by the dramatist, it is vital to be able to discuss and analyse the play from a variety of different perspectives.

Notwithstanding this observation, it is also important to recognise that, for actors, the task of researching a play does not mean preparing to write an essay or give a seminar presentation. Rather than serve essentially theoretical aspirations, an actor's preparation for a role must ultimately be directed at the artistic aims for which the play was originally conceived. In other words, actors need to *perform* in the plays they study and it is important, therefore, to ensure that the methods used for undertaking research are suited to this *practical* outcome.

It was with this precise aim in mind that Stanislavski developed his technique of dividing the play into small 'units of action'. Just as we wouldn't attempt to consume an entire meal in one mouthful, preferring instead to cut each portion into smaller morsels that are then flavoured and slowly chewed and digested, so we shouldn't seek to 'devour' a whole play at a single reading. To fully appreciate all of the subtleties and variations that the play makes available, it is necessary to break it into smaller segments that are then examined in close detail through discussion *and* action. Generally speaking, an actor's 'units of action', do not always coincide with the scenic divisions that may have been used by the playwright. Instead, each scene is divided into a series of smaller individual components. Each component encapsulates a 'unit of action' and starts and begins whenever the action is changed or altered in some way. For instance, in a scene involving two characters locked in an intimate discussion, a change in the topic of conversation, the departure of one character, the arrival of a new one or a sudden shift in the given circumstances will generally mark the end of one component and the beginning of another.

By going through each scene and dividing it into 'units of action' in this way, a performer can begin to acquire a strong practical sense of the overall structure of the play. In order to prevent the possibility of becoming overloaded with too many units or with too much unhelpful detail, it will prove beneficial to pick out some of the drama's key components along the way. Perhaps the best way of doing this is to locate the foundation on which the play is established – the thing without which it would not exist. In Shakespeare's *Macbeth*, for example, we can say that without the determination of the two central characters to become Scotland's rulers and the horrific acts of murder that are instigated in order for them to achieve and then to retain their hold on power, much of what else happens in the play would prove nonsensical. By comparing the work of an actor to that of an airline pilot that determines his route through a series of unmistakable landmarks, Stanislavski emphasises the need for economy:

'So an actor must proceed, not by a multitude of details, but by those important units which, like signals, mark his channel and keep him in the right creative line.' (27)

An Actor Prepares by Konstantin Stanislavski

Having identified a series of 'units', it is then useful to label each one in such a way as to begin to trace an outline of the developing action. This process is invaluable in that, if it is done with sensitivity and care, it can reveal objectives for each of the characters that appear in the scene – not all of which will be the same!

It is this particular feature of the uniting process that imparts one of the most dynamic and creative elements to an actor's interpretation of the dramatic action. By choosing and playing out *objectives* that are coherent with the movement of each scene, the given circumstances and the characters relationships, the actor will begin to reveal the multifarious meanings – both internal and external – that the play makes available.

The term *objective* is used to describe the things that the character desires, needs or strives to achieve. It provides the justification for all of the character's physical actions and in so doing locates both psychological and emotional needs. Although it is customary to speak of objectives in physical terms, it is most important to recognise that both the psychological and physical dimensions of a character's desires are inextricably linked. In choosing a character's objective, therefore, it is important to bear in mind the degree to which it reflects both the inner and outer needs.

Whereas it is perfectly acceptable to use a noun when labelling a unit – eg *The Arrival* or *The Discovery* – it is important to use an active verb when identifying which objective to play in a given scene. This helps to animate dramatic action and drive the play forward. To ensure that each objective is as dynamic and attractive to the actor as possible, it is helpful to ask 'What do I want?' The answer to this question needs to be as precise as possible if it is to stimulate the imagination in such a way as to initiate action of some kind. Hence whilst an answer such as 'I want her to stay' might offer a somewhat vague indication of a character's need, the statement 'I want to make her change her mind! I want to make her understand how much I love her! I want to let her see how guilty I have been feeling and how much I regret my actions; I want to urge her to give our relationship another chance' helps to provoke the imagination in a much more urgent and compelling way. In addition, therefore, to identifying what it is that a character wants during a given sequence, it can also help to sharpen the objective if a response is found to the additional question: 'What do I need *to do* in order to get the thing that I want?' The emphasis on the need *to do* something is important, since acting necessarily involves action of some kind.

To guide the actor in arriving at appropriate and playable objectives, Stanislavski provides the following criteria that can be used as a means of assessing the efficacy of the creative choices that are made:

1 The actor must ensure that the objective is directed at the other actor(s) in the scene rather than at the audience.

2 The objective must draw from the actor's own personal experience – his/her emotion memory whilst at the same time being analogous to the experiences of the character.

3 The objective must be the product of creative and artistic investigation. It must provide the basis for offering a profound insight into human behaviour.

4 Every objective must be based in real human experience rather than drawn from cliché or tired theatrical convention.

5 The choice of objective must have a strong sense of integrity and truth so that both the spectator and the other actors in the scene can believe in it.

6   The actor must be attracted to the objective – it must prove stimulating and exciting to the individual actor and provoke the imagination.

7   The choice of objective must be extremely detailed and appropriate to the personality of the character, the given circumstances and the socio-historic environment in which the play is situated.

8   The objective must be connected to the inner life of the character. It must be meaningful and have the potential to reflect complex psychological impulses.

9   The objective must be dynamic and forward moving. It must serve to advance the action of the play.

Although this list might initially strike us as being somewhat demanding or unnecessarily detailed, a careful consideration of each point will prove invaluable in enabling an actor to make informed, creative choices that will serve to empower and enrich the rehearsal process.

Having carefully united the play and selected appropriate and playable objectives for the character, the next stage is to begin to experiment with different ways of achieving the desired objective. What changes need to be made – to the tone of voice, the expression in the eyes, the way in which the text is delivered? If the objective is to be fully realised, then it will necessitate a series of adjustments in the character's behaviour. These adjustments, or 'adaptations' (28) as Stanislavski refers to them, are the means that an actor uses in order to realise the character's objectives.

Although there is a tendency in modern teaching/rehearsal practice to replace the word *adaptation* with *activity*, *action* or *tactic*, it is important, at the outset, to recognise that none of these words accurately capture the numerous ideas that Stanislavski attributes to the concept of *adaptation*. For th purposes of the present discussion, therefore, the original Stanislavski term will be used. Although the meanings of the other words are far from interchangeable with Stanislavski's, everything that pertains to the term *adaptation* can be applied in more or less equal measure to any of the alternative ways of describing the general concept.

For Stanislavski, the term *adaptation* is used to describe *'the inner and outer human means that people use in adjusting themselves to one another in a variety of relationships and also as an aid in affecting an object'*(29).Whilst in many circumstances adaptations are employed as a means of enabling the achievement of chosen objectives, they can also be used to draw attention to inner feelings, alter the mood of a partner, change the atmosphere in a given scene, or even to express unspoken thoughts and impulses. The most important feature of this aspect of the System is that it insists on the need for the actor to adjust his/her behaviour on stage in such a way as to remain extremely sensitive to all of the other elements that make up the scene. In much the same way that our behaviour in real life is shaped by an awareness of those around us – how they feel about certain things, their personality traits, their moods – so too should an actor's behaviour be similarly influenced when creating convincing stage relationships. Indeed, rather than assume that instinctive adjustments in behaviour can be taken for granted, an actor needs to become acutely aware of their effect in order to maximise on the creative opportunities that such changes can afford.

'If people in ordinary walks of life need and make use of a large variety of adaptations, actors need a correspondingly greater number because we must be constantly in contact with one another and therefore incessantly adjusting ourselves.'(30)

An Actor Prepares by Konstantin Stanislavski

The choice of which *adaptation* to use at a given point is determined by all of the surrounding circumstances, the personalities, moods and interests of the other people in the scene, and the character's own disposition. For this reason it is necessary to experiment with many different *adaptations* before selecting which are best suited both to the choice of objective and the nature of the scenic relationship.

Let us assume, for instance, that an actor, having undertaken a close analysis of a scene and divided it into units of action, has chosen to play the following scenic objective:

> 'I want to make her change her mind! I want to make her understand how much I love her! I want to let her see how guilty I have been feeling and how much I regret my actions; I want to urge her to give our relationship another chance.'

If I am to achieve my *objective* I need to bring about a change in the way my partner is feeling and behaving towards me. In order to do this I might begin by exploring any of the following as the basis for an *adaptation*.

- I will make my partner feel sorry for me.

- I will make her feel guilty about the apparent ease with which she can simply abandon our relationship.

- I will remind her of all the good times we have had together and how fantastically well suited we are.

- I will warn her of the consequences if she does leave and make it clear to her that she can never ever come back.

When working with and experimenting with *adaptations*, it is important to ensure that they engage the actor physically s that the scene remains 'spontaneous' and 'active' rather tha merely intellectual. If we were to reduce each of the above *adaptations* to a sequence of single words, we would arrive at something like SORROWFUL, GUILTY, SENTIMENTAL and CAUTIOUS. In order to produce such different feelings in my partner, it is necessary to make very significant adjustments in my behaviour. Moreover, if my partner is to believe in the things I am saying and doing, it is imperative that they also reflect my inner thoughts and feelings.

Whilst the use of *adaptation* adds variety and dynamism to stage relationships, it is important to ensure that they are played in such a way as to enable the achievement of the desired objective rather than simply for their own sake. Their function is to aid the development of dramatic action in a way that is entirely coherent with the nature of each relationship, the given circumstances and the logic that informs the play itself.

If the practice of *uniting* enables the actor to understand the overall structure of a play and identifying *objectives* and *adaptations* provides a framework in which to translate this understanding into dramatic action, then the function of *super-objective* is to give resonance and meaning to all of the processes that an actor undertakes in creating a role. All of the imaginative insights, the individual traits and feelings that make up the personality of the character, the choice of objectives and tactics, the relationships both to events and other characters, must all converge so as to realise what Stanislavski refers to as *'the super-objective of the plot'* (31).

Generally speaking the term *super-objective* is used to describe and encapsulate the essence of what we feel the play is about – the catalyst or impetus which animates the action and gives the play its driving force. The right choice of *super-objective* serves to focus all of the creative energy that is directed at the play and allows both the director and the performers to trace a logical and coherent through line for the drama as it unfolds. Without this essential cohesive element the finished product is in danger of appearing disparate and inconsistent.

Alongside the need to identify a *super-objective* for the drama as a whole, it is also enormously beneficial to choose one for each character in the play. Aside from helping to enhance the degree of consistency and logic in relation to an individual actor's interpretative choices, such a procedure highlights significant moments of tension and areas of conflict – a feature that is essential to all good drama! However, in making decisions about which *super-objectives* to use for individual characters, it is most important not to undermine the integrity of the one which has been chosen to represent the artistic endeavours of the entire company.

Perhaps, not surprisingly, making good decisions in relation to *super-objectives* is far from easy. For this reason it is often best to delay making a choice until all of the actors and the director feel they have reached the stage at which they are extremely familiar with the play and with the different relationships and situations that it presents. At least when this stage has been reached it is possible to explore a wide range of opinion and insight that has been gleaned from the *practical* investigations that have taken place during the course of rehearsal.

Although, in the previous quotation, Stanislavski's use of the word *'plot'* might encourage the belief that the *super-objective* must be derived from the playwright's intentions, it is not unusual in more contemporary practice to relocate the rationale informing the choice of a *super-objective* so as to reflect the interpretative vision of the director, for instance, or even the artistic aims of a particular ensemble. Ultimately, whatever guiding principle is used to determine the choice of a play's *super-objective*, the important thing is to ensure that it imparts a strong sense of cohesiveness, logic and consistenc in relation to all of the elements that contribute to the ongoing development of the dramatic action.

In order to develop the ability to unit a play and identify appropriate and playable objectives, it will prove rewarding to undertake some of the following exercises:

- Select a two or three hour period in your recent past in which you were engaged in a series of activities that were directed towards a specific goal. In preparation for a party, for instance, you might have washed your hair, ironed your clothes and wrapped a present. Having identified such an event write down all the details – everything you did, felt and thought during the period in question. When you have completed this task, try to imagine that this episode in your life formed part of a scene in a play. Now go through the scene carefully and divide it into *units of action*. How many units have you identified? What name would you give to each unit?

- Working with a partner, select a small extract from a play that you know well and featuring characters with which you are both familiar. See if you can pick out individual *units of action* in the chosen extract. The focus on this exercise should be on the development of the story – the relationships and events that it depicts rather than the inner feelings of the character. Give each unit a title and try to ensure that each title captures the essence of the unit in question.

- Having completed this stage, revisit the units to try and identify individual objectives for each character. What does each character want in the scene? Try to keep the objectives simple to start with and focus only on what the character *wants* or *needs* in the given extract.

- When each participant has identified what each character wants from the given scene, try to express each objective in the form of a statement of some kind. Use Stanislavski's list of criteria as a guide and ensure that all of the requirements are met. Compare your statement with that of your partner – is there a conflict of some kind?

- The next stage is to identify what needs to be done in order to achieve the chosen objective. What *adaptations* might need to be introduced to the scene? It will be helpful to make as full a list of *adaptations* as possible at this stage so that when it comes to rehearsing the scene you will have lots of ideas to experiment with.

- Now begin rehearsing the scene with a partner and start to test out both of your ideas and a range of different *adaptations* in order to realise your objectives.

- Finally, when both of you feel that you know the play well and have a sense of the way in which all of the events serve to make up the essence of the play as a whole, try to formulate at least three possible *super-objectives* that could be used as a basis for rehearsal. Which one is best and why?

There is no doubt that taking the trouble to work on a play in this way produces enormous benefits and allows an actor to adopt an extremely detailed and imaginative approach to rehearsal. Initially, identifying *units of action*, *objectives*, *adaptations* and *super-objectives* can seem quite daunting but with patience, dedication, practice and careful guidance it can become a natural and indispensable part of an actor's creative process.

A Sense of Transformation

If an actor is to achieve a genuinely convincing vocal and physical transformation, then it is necessary to begin to find ways of producing changes in one's own natural tempo and rhythm. It is often the case that inexperienced actors will become disillusioned when, despite all of their best efforts in every other aspect of the creative work that has been undertaken, they are unable to *feel* like the character. This absence of a complete sense of transformation is often due to a failure to understand the need to adjust the tempo-rhythms of the performer to those of the character. Consequently, all of their movements and actions, the speed and quality of the voice and their inner responses remain unchanged, thereby producing a feeling of frustration and unease.

In all of the activities we undertake on a daily basis, whether travelling to work, relaxing in the bath, or taking exercise there are constant changes in our tempo-rhythm. Even in those moments when we appear to be absolutely still – as in prayer, or when we are locked in deep thought, for instance – there are constant variations in the speed and intensity of our thoughts and movements.

Stanislavski defines *tempo* as the speed or slowness of our movements and *rhythm* as the force and intensity behind them. Importantly, when thinking about producing variations in *tempo-rhythm,* it is essential not to lose sight of the extent to which such changes affect our inner lives.

'In a word tempo-rhythm carries with itself not only external qualities which directly affect our natures, but also our inner content which nourishes our feelings. In

this guise tempo-rhythm remains in our memories and may be used for creative purposes.' (32)

> *Building a Character* by Konstantin Stanislavski

If we bring to mind the experience of having witnessed a funeral, for instance, or being involved in an emergency of some kind, we will instantly recall and tune into startling differences in the *tempo-rhythm* of each event. Similarly if we listen to and compare different kinds of music – for example, rock music and an operatic aria – we will experience differences in the speed, variation and intensity of each piece. The same can also be said about the things that we see and feel; a calm sea or a powerful thunder storm will produce different *tempo-rhythms* to those of a road accident or a gentle, warm breeze. In all of these instances, the physical changes we experience are matched by alterations in mood or emotional energy. How many of us feel gladdened by the arrival of summer, for example, or experience anxiety during the long dark evenings of winter?

Just as external influences produce changes in our physical behaviour, so too do the things we experience and feel internally. By stimulating our visual memories to bring past images to life it is possible to completely alter both the way we behave and the emotions we experience.

> *'Listen to how your emotions tremble, throb, race, are stirred inside you. In these invisible movements lie hidden all manner of rapid and slow beats… Every human passion, every state of being, every experience has its tempo-rhythms. Every characteristic inner or outer external image has its own tempo-rhythm.'* (33)

> *Building a Character* by Konstantin Stanislavski

In order to produce a convincing transformation into the life of the character, an actor needs to be able to locate the variations in *tempo-rhythm* that occur through each stage of the play. Alongside a careful consideration of the given circumstances, the character's personality traits, the nature of each relationship and the objectives and adaptations the actor has chosen to play, an examination of those moments involving conflict or struggle of some kind will help the actor to tune into different patterns of physical and emotional behaviour. How does my *tempo-rhythm* change when I am in physical danger, or when I am confronting a much feared enemy, or betraying a friend?

An understanding of *tempo-rhythm* can help the actor bridge the gap between the inner and outer realms of experience. Often, the source of conflict is located not in other people and events but in the character him/herself. Macbeth's growing paranoia and furious temper, for instance, spring more from his own sense of guilt and attacks of conscience than from any external source. It can be helpful, therefore, when working on physical *tempo-rhythm* to explore the extent to which the outward behaviour runs counter to what the character feels or desires internally.

In the same way that changes in *tempo-rhythm* affect the way we move, they also produce changes in the way that we speak – the words that we use, the way in which we phrase things, even the sounds of the words themselves. Indeed, in spoken language, it is the structure and arrangements of the sounds and syllables that help to convey an additional layer of meaning. In other words, it isn't just what we say that is important, but also how we say it!

If the speed at which we speak marks the *tempo* of our utterances, the manner in which we punctuate the things we say – how often we pause, the emphasis we give at certain points and the adjustments in tone and volume – imparts sense of *rhythm* to the things we say. In accordance with alterations in situation and circumstance, both of these things can change considerably. Notice, for instance, the way in which the *tempo-rhythm* of a TV news presenter's speech will change when relaying news of a grave and serious nature as opposed to something of a more light-hearted vein that typically appears towards the end of the programme.

Whereas the use of verse and carefully chosen imagery in a play can make it much easier for an actor to tune into the changes and shifts that occur in spoken language, the same is not true of prose. This isn't to claim, however, that a play written in prose lacks *tempo-rhythm*; on the contrary, the reverse is true:

> *'There is tempo-rhythm in prose as well as in poetry and music. But in ordinary speech it is accidental. In prose the tempo-rhythm is mixed: one phrase will be spoken in one rhythm, the next in an entirely different one. One phrase will be long, another short, and each will have its own particular rhythm'*(34)

> *Building a Character* by Konstantin Stanislavski

By alternating patterns of stressed and unstressed vowels and consonants and learning to vary the speed and quality with which the words themselves are delivered, an actor can produce very significant shifts and alterations in the *tempo-rhythm* of a character's speech.

As with *tempo-rhythm* of movement, such changes prompt a whole series of internal responses that can serve to connect the actor to the inner feelings and emotional experiences of the character. Like movement, the *tempo-rhythms* produced by speech can have a profound effect on the way we feel internally. The realisation that millions of theatre-goers all over the world are regularly moved and delighted at performances of plays that are in languages that they do not understand bears testimony to this fact. In such instances, it can't be the words and speeches in and of themselves that have affected the audience, but rather the ability of the performers to locate and give expression to the constantly shifting *tempo-rhythms* of the linguistic exchanges.

In order to become sensitised to all of the possibilities that speech affords the actor, it is necessary to pay careful attention to words. The thoughts and images they can evoke, the sounds they make individually and when grouped together, the powers they have to provoke both physical and silent responses in the listener, their ability to express the way we feel and make ourselves understood. In most instances, words come to the actor in the form of a written script, so an actor needs to acquire the additional skill of learning to read and make sense of punctuation. Aside from guiding the reader, and by implication the listener, as to the meaning of the words that appear in the text, punctuation can also offer an indication of how to interpret the words – where to pause or hesitate, whether to speak in short, fast bursts or long, ponderous ones, or whether to stress a key point or skip over it.

In both *An Actor Prepares* and *Building a Character* all of the students that attend Tortsov's acting classes also take part in regular movement and voice sessions. The chief function of these is to develop discipline, muscularity, sensitivity and expressiveness in both the voice and the body. If an actor is to become acutely aware of how to tune into and change the *tempo-rhythm* of both voice and movement, it will be necessary to attend regular classes with specialised tutors over a sustained period of time. Indeed, many actors never reach the stage where they feel ready to give up voice and movement classes, preferring instead to continue to perfect their ability to convey even the most subtle aspects of human behaviour with ever-increasing precision and clarity.

In order to begin the process of becoming sensitive to changes in *tempo-rhythm*, it will prove rewarding to take part in the following exercises:

- Select two pieces of contrasting music. Listen to each one in turn and begin to feel the ways in which it affects your *tempo-rhythm*. Rather than become fixated by the music, it is often a good idea to listen to it when you are physically involved in performing another task – eg doing the washing-up or cooking a meal. Try not to become too self-conscious, instead relax and let the music affect you. In what ways does the music influence the speed and intensity of your movements? What physical and internal changes do you notice in the way that each piece of music affects you?

- Develop the above exercise in such a way as to find a justification for your movements. If the music increases and lightens your *tempo-rhythm*, give yourself a justification for this change. For instance, imagine you have organised a surprise birthday party for a loved one. The house is full of guests and you have just heard that s/he is at the end of the road and will arrive in one minute.

- Repeat the above exercise finding justifications for a whole range of shifts in inner and outer *tempo-rhythm*.

- Closely observe somebody whom you believe to embody a very different *tempo-rhythm* to your own – either much faster and lighter or much slower and heavier or any combination of these. See if you can absorb a similar *tempo-rhythm* yourself whilst finding an inner justification for the change. Maintain the new *tempo-rhythm* whilst performing a series of different tasks eg eating, shaving, walking to work. What changes do you notice both internally and externally?

- Sitting or lying down in a comfortable position, try to picture yourself in a series of different environments. You might, for example, imagine that you are in the middle of a long overdue confrontation with someone who has continuously abused you. Alternatively, you might imagine going on a first date with someone that you have admired from a distance, but have been too afraid to approach. Try to be as creative as possible in the choice of situation and ensure that each one is different. Following each situation, spend a few moments analysing both your inner and outer *tempo-rhythm*. What changes can you detect in your breathing or pulse rate? Has your mood or emotional energy changed?

- Examine an extract from a novel that you know well. Pay close attention to all of the punctuation and mark any particular shifts in emphasis or mood. Invite a friend to listen whilst you read the extract aloud. How well have you communicated the content of the extract? Repeat the reading a second time only on this occasion rearrange the speed and intensity of your delivery in such a way as to alter the *tempo-rhythm* of the extract without losing the general sense of what is being communicated. How difficult did you find this task? How would you begin to describe the changes in each of the readings? In what ways did these changes alter or affect the way in which your partner listened to the extract?

- Repeat the same exercise, except on this occasion select an extract that contains a great deal of complicated or technical information that you do not understand. If you feel particularly confident about your ability to pronounce unfamiliar words or phrases, choose an extract from a foreign newspaper.

Go through exactly the same process as the previous exercise. In what ways did your changes in *tempo-rhythm* serve to convey different meanings to the extract? Did they produce alterations in the way that either the listener or yourself related to the text?

- Working with a partner, choose a short extract from a play that alternates a series of four or five brief exchanges. Having made some decisions about the relationship and the given circumstances begin to read and re-read the text to each other whilst changing the speed and pattern of stresses in each line. Try to find an inner justification for each change. How many variations can you come up with? What are the effects of these – on the individual and the relationship?

- Repeat the above exercise with music playing in the background. It is important to let the music establish itself and affect you before starting to read the scene. What changes occur if the music is played gently, loudly or if it is changed completely? Try to combine shifts in the *tempo-rhythm* of speech with simultaneous changes in the body as a whole. What happens if the scene is performed whilst dancing to loud music in a park or when hearing distant music whilst locked in a dark and extremely small cupboard?

When working on a play it is possible to experiment with limitless combinations and arrangements of tempo and rhythm. The important thing is to ensure that whatever combinations are finally chosen, they produce transformations that will ultimately enable the actor to make sense of the play's action and give clear and unambiguous expression to the ideas it embodies.

Conclusion

In light of all of the elements that have been examined in the preceding discussion, it would seem reasonable to claim that in developing his System for actors, Stanislavski succeeded in making a hugely significant contribution not just to our understanding of the actor's creative process, but also to the nature of theatre art in general.

Whereas previous generations of actors were expected to learn their craft from observing and imitating more experienced and often less accomplished performers, actors of today are afforded the comparative luxury of being able to experiment with and test out all of the techniques Stanislavski makes available in the relative safety of a classroom or rehearsal studio before being exposed to an audience. In providing the means for the actor to become self-consciously aware of the creative processes by which dramatic characters and relationships are created, the System has enabled actors to elevate their craft from that of a hackneyed collection of vaudevillian clichés into a detailed and highly fascinating art form.

Although, during the course of the discussion, each element of the System has been analysed separately and in close detail, it is important to bear in mind that the efficacy of the approach that Stanislavski advocates hinges on the mutual dependence and interplay between each of the various components. The System is entirely holistic and any attempt to fragment the ideas it expresses into discrete entities will greatly diminish its impact.

Of equal importance is the need to recognise that far from bringing his System to a stage of 'completeness' or 'closure', Stanislavski continued experimenting with new ideas until the end of his life. The highly organic and 'live' nature of the techniques that he developed draw their dynamism and potency from their ability to enable the actor to reflect human behaviour in all of its various guises. To attempt to suggest, therefore, that the System embodies a fully formed and complete methodology ignores the fact that human behaviour is in a constant state of flux. Indeed, one of the greatest advantages that Stanislavski's approach affords actors is its ability to constantly adapt and measure the affects it produces against the world it seeks to represent.

Whilst it is certainly true that the principles on which the System is based are predicated on certain assumptions about human experience – that character is knowable and can be clearly defined, that personality is stable, that experience is linear and that ideas about the relationship between inner and outer experience are shared across different nationalities and cultures – this is no reason to cast doubt on its efficacy.

Notwithstanding the tenets of postmodernism and its rejection of the notion of a stable and knowable universe, one of the consequences of the way in which language shapes our experience of the world and our ability to engage with it, is its tendency to produce an undeniable sense of unity and order. Whatever form our intellectual deliberations about the nature of memory, habit, psychology and identity may take, our practical and daily experience of these aspects of human nature are likely, for the foreseeable future at least, to remain somewhat similar to those described by Stanislavski. It seems entirely appropriate, therefore, for actors and directors alike to continue to explore, test out, adapt and reformulate one of the most profoundly influential systems of artistic representation ever to have been produced.

DISCUSSION POINTS

- Recall a play that you have seen recently. With reference to some of the techniques described above, begin to offer an account of the actors' performances. Which aspects stood out as being particularly strong or convincing and which were less satisfying?

- Stanislavski's approach to acting is predicated on the belief that it is possible to describe and predict human behaviour in close detail. Do you agree that this is the case? What evidence would you use to support your argument?

- To what extent does Stanislavski's approach make it possible for an actor to become aware of the quality of his/her own acting? How far does the 'System' serve to empower those who adopt the principles it advocates?

- Would you say that Stanislavski's System is equally well suited to both theatre and film? What evidence can you draw on to support your point of view?

- Many theatre practitioners have argued that rather than use the stage as a mirror on which to reflect our daily lives, or to confirm the things that we already know about ourselves, it should be used as a means of provoking change or highlighting, as yet, unrealised potential. Do you agree with this view? What arguments can you use to support your point of view?

- Do you believe that the techniques originally pioneered by Stanislavski are as relevant today as they were when they were initially conceived? What evidence can you draw on to support your views?

Bibliography and Further Reading

Primary Sources

Stanislavski, K. – *An Actor Prepares* (translated by Elizabeth Reynolds Hapgood). Methuen, 1986 (1937)

Stanislavski, K. – *Building a Character* (translated by Elizabeth Reynolds Hapgood). Routledge, 1994 (1949)

Stanislavski, K. – *Stanislavski on the Art of the Stage* (translated by David Magarshack). Faber and Faber Ltd, 1967 (1950)

Stanislavski, K. – *Creating a Role* (translated by Elizabeth Reynolds Hapgood). Methuen, 1984 (1961)

Stanislavski, K. – *An Actor's Handbook* (translated by Elizabeth Reynolds Hapgood). Methuen, 1990

Secondary Sources

Benedetti, J. – *Stanislavski: A Biography.* Methuen, 1988

Benedetti, J. – *Stanislavski and the Actor.* Methuen, 1998

Carnicke, S.M. – '*Stanislavski's System: Pathways for the Actor*', reprinted in Hodge, A. – *Twentieth Century Actor Training.* Routledge, 2000

Merlin, B. – *Konstantin Stanislavski.* Routledge, 2003

Moore, S. – *The Stanislavski System: The Professional Training of an Actor.* Penguin, 1984 (1965)

Wells, Stanley and Taylor, Gary (eds.) – *William Shakespeare – The Complete Works.* OUP, 1986

Notes and References

(1) Stanislavski, K. – *An Actor Prepares* (translated by Elizabeth Reynolds Hapgood). Methuen, 1986

(2) *Ibid*

(3) *Ibid*

(4) *Ibid*

(5) *Ibid*

(6) *Ibid*

(7) *Ibid*

(8) *Ibid*

(9) *Ibid*

(10) *Ibid*

(11) *Ibid*

(12) *Ibid*

(13) *Ibid*

(14) *Ibid*

(15) *Ibid*

(16) *Ibid*

(17) *Ibid*

(18) *Ibid*

(19) *Ibid*

(20) *Ibid*

(21) *Ibid*

(22) *Ibid*

(23) *Ibid*

(24) *Ibid*

(25) *Ibid*

(26) *Ibid*

(27) *Ibid*

(28) *Ibid*

(29) *Ibid*

(30) *Ibid*

(31) *Ibid*

(32) Stanislavski, K. – *Building a Character* (translated by Elizabeth Reynolds Hapgood). Routledge, 1994

(33) *Ibid*

(34) *Ibid*

Chapter Two

Laban:
His Contribution to the Art
and Craft of the Actor

by

Penny Cherns

Introduction

I trained at the Drama Centre in London, where I was taught *Movement Psychology* by Yat Malmgren, based on the work of Rudolf von Laban and William Carpenter. I found this work revelatory and subsequently have seen it used in various formats in many trainings and with differing levels of understanding and appreciation.

It is the extraordinary genesis of Laban's work and the crucible from which his work emerged that gives it such depth. It overlaps with so many movers and shakers in the world of dance and drama in the 20th Century that it is useful to disentangle his contribution and then weave it back in.

The catalogue of the Modernism exhibition, *1914-1939 Designing a New World*, notes an upsurge in physical and *'active body culture'* during that period because of the *'disenchantment with traditional intellectual culture'*(1). Part of this could be seen in the extraordinary explosion of *'a dance tradition separate from ballet, concerned with free movement, abstraction and spirituality'*(2).

The link between physical expression and inner emotional content had a trajectory reaching back into the 18th Century: Denis Diderot (1713-1781) explored the connection, which was later codified by Francois Delsarte (1811-1871). Delsarte trained as an actor and singer, performing as a tenor with the *Opera Comique* and subsequently becoming a vocal coach. His methods linked voice and gesture, based on the observation of thousands of everyday gestures. The dancer Isadora Duncan, studied with him as did F.M. Alexander, the creator of the Alexander technique.

Meanwhile, Emile Jacques-Dalcroze (1865-1950) founded a school of movement education which explored connections with the harmony of nature: his analytical method of movement, based on musical rhythm, was called *Eurythmics*. Mary Wigman (1886-1973), who was one of the most important influences on modern American dance, studied with him briefly; she later collaborated with Rudolf von Laban.

Jacques Copeau (1879-1949) experimented with *Eurythmics* but, like Laban, felt that it didn't connect with the inner emotions: he sought to train an expressive actor rather than a dancer, which revolutionised actor training. His pupil, Etienne Decroux (1898-1991), developed corporeal mime, using the human body as the main means of expression and he taught, among others, the mime artist Marcel Marceau.

The catalogue of the Modernism Exhibition indicates a tremendous overlap between artists (Kandinsky, Nolde), architects (Mies van der Rohe, Le Corbusier), musicians and the new movement and dance techniques. It offers an extraordinary sense of artists moving in and out of each others' ideas, dipping in, exploring, creating, searching for ways to free ideas; a hunt for internal and external expression; and a desire to find the spiritual, the meaningful. Central to this overlap was the establishment of a centre at Monte Verita in Ascona, Switzerland, in 1900, where a community sought alternative ways of living and where Laban explored and developed his work. A reaction to the rationalisation, industrialisation and mechanisation of the late 19th Century, it attracted writers, philosophers, artists and psychiatrists, as well as many proponents of body culture, from naturism to dance.

At one end of the spectrum was the idea of correct posture, which focused on understanding the movement of the body in daily activities. Then there was sport and gymnastics, leading to the construction of huge sport stadiums across Europe and at the other end was the growth of freedom and self-expression; the spiritual freeing of dance from classical ballet. The hunt for inner life, expressive clarity, functional pareness and truth, which informed Laban's work, was born out of this inter-war zeitgeist. He overlapped and worked with many important and experimental artists of the late 19th and 20th Centuries.

Laban

Rudolf von Laban was born in Bratislava, which was then in Austria-Hungary (now Slovakia) in 1879. Although his father, who was the military governor of the area then known as Bosnia-Herzegovina, wanted him to be in the military as befitted his social standing and background, he chose to be an artist. He studied in Munich, which was then an artistic melting pot, and subsequently moved to Paris.

He saw Isadora Duncan perform there and wrote:

> '...there was no story behind her dances, which were, as she herself termed it, the expression of the life of her 'soul'... At a time when science, and especially psychology, endeavoured to abolish radically any notion of a 'soul'. This dancer had the courage to demonstrate successfully that there exists in the flow of man's movement some ordering principle which cannot be explained in the usual rationalistic manner' (3).

In 1904 he returned to Munich, having found it difficult to study and subsist in Paris, and started to focus on physical culture through dance, having already studied under Delsarte. He designed costumes and did some choreography for the 1911-1912 carnival season in Schwabing (a bohemian part of Munich) and began to develop a reputation for new and exciting work in movement and choreography. Wassily Kandinsky's treatise, *Concerning the Spirituality of Art*, inspired him and he came into contact with the work of Dalcroze. However he diverged from both Delsarte and Dalcroze by throwing away structure and the need for music or any external rhythm becoming interested in how dance movement originated from the inside, the 'inner attitude' of the dancer, which, he felt, changed the nature and dynamic of a dancer's movement. This was to become one of his key concepts.

His work on the carnival was exhausting and so he travelled to the White Deer sanatorium near Dresden to recuperate, where, amongst others, he met Suzanne Perrottet. She had taught at the Dalcroze Institute and helped him to define his developing ideas of movement analysis. After the sanatorium they travelled together to the community of Monte Verita in Ancona, choosing to live in neutral Switzerland during World War I. In 1917 he moved to Zurich and set up an Art of Movement School, devising a curriculum and new terminology with the help of Mary Wigman, who eventually became one of the most profound influences on modern American dance.

At the end of the war he returned to Germany where he met Kurt Jooss, who became his student and artistic collaborator and eventually founded the Ballets Jooss. In Stuttgart, Laban invented his ideas about choreutics and worked to increase the status of dance but, under the Nazis, this status declined and new dance ideas were stifled. He was placed under house arrest, then arrested, and finally smuggled out to Paris and brought to England.

In England his work took new directions. Through Kurt Jooss and Lisa Ullman (who had smuggled some of his papers out of Germany) he was introduced to Dartington Hall. He wrote, he and Ullman taught, and his ideas became accepted in educational fields. He wrote a book about modern educational dance, published in 1948, and this work was supported and acted on by local education authorities in the Fifties, although subsequently subsumed into physical education. He then worked with Frederick Lawrence as part of a national drive to make work life more efficient during World War II. Lawrence was a management consultant, who encouraged him to use his notation and analysis to help industrial efficiency. Laban's observations on effort in work however, clearly illustrate his thinking about natural and expressive movement. He moved to Manchester to undertake this work and began the Art of Movement Studio where Joan Littlewood, the founder of the groundbreaking Theatre Workshop, regularly sent her actors to train.

Parallel with these developments, Anny Boalth, who had been a student of Laban's in Hamburg, brought his work to the Royal Academy of Dramatic Art (RADA). This was continued by Yat Malmgren, who had worked with the Ballets Jooss. He explored principles that Laban began investigating with William Carpenter, linking Laban's movement analyses to psychological processes, which he took to the Drama Centre in London. Through serendipity and a constant need to explore and experiment, and through the insight of his collaborators and students, Laban's work became central to the art and craft of the actor. He seemed to knit together and touch upon many of the ideas and explorations bubbling through the early 20th Century.

The three major areas of Laban's work were, therefore, in education (including industry), dance and theatre, where he recognised an emotional inner life, mediated through the mind and expressed in movement. However, he was constantly evolving his ideas, which is why its offshoots have taken so many different directions. The work can, of course, be used and studied discretely, but it is also important to view its historical context, the spirit of exploration and artistic hunger that it grew out of and the cross references to other artists of the period in order to understand Laban's belief in the human potential.

Movement

Laban's ideas about social dance were developed to counteract the perception of movement as being merely a part of physical culture. He felt that creative movement, as shown in community and national dancing, touched deeper levels, and created movement choirs, exploring his conviction that there is an interdependence of body, mind and spirit.

In his preface to *The Mastery of Movement on the Stage* Laban wrote:

> 'The source whence perfection and final mastery of movement must flow is the understanding of that part of the inner life of man where movement and action originate......There exists an almost mathematical relationship between the inner motivation of movement and the functions of the body; and guidance in the knowledge and application of the common principles of impulse and function is the only means that can promote the freedom and spontaneity of the moving person'(4).
> And 'Movement has always been used for two distinct aims: the attainment of tangible values in all kinds of work, and the approach to intangible values in prayer and worship. The same bodily movements have always been used in work and worship, but the significance of the movement is different.'(5)

The overlap between the tangible and the intangible is at the centre of Laban's work. A movement can be made for an obvious and visible reason – for instance, to reach for something – but it can also be the outward manifestation of an inner impulse, something invisible. If you watch someone chopping wood, the chopping action is clear; but that same physical action can be seen – without the axe or the wood – in the hand gestures of someone talking. If you try out the gesture for yourself then you may discover how often you use it and the context in which you use it. This is what Laban was attempting to analyse: what inner impulse might provide that outer physical gesture – an action that, in its energy and dynamic, matches an action used at work, that is, a *working action*. Therefore, there is an overlap between the idea of *working* movement – a movement made for a reason – and *expressive* movement – which may look the same but has no obvious outer reason. This idea lies behind his concept of *working actions*.

Laban was keen to find ways of recording that dynamic and was involved in notating it from the beginning of his career. He called it *Kinetography* but it is now more widely known as *Labannotation* and it is a way of recording not only the origin of the movement but its dynamic properties.

Laban movement is obviously a great training for dancers but it is also a splendid method of opening up avenues to physical improvisation. It functions as a way of locating the performer's own physical habits, allowing them to move away from their own centre to find a character. However, it can also be applied directly to text and language. There are clues in the shape, rhythm and feel of the text that gives the actor clues to the inner and outer life of a character. This was the work Laban was involved in developing towards the end of his life.

Concepts

Movement happens to satisfy a need. Laban wrote: *'It is the result of striving after an object deemed valuable, or of a state of mind'* (6). It is coloured by the environment, a situation, a place, an epoch: it is heightened by interaction, offering and receiving; it is influenced by motivation and choice, distinguishing humans from animals. *'No-one has ever seen a cat strut with a horse-like gait. A catlike man, however, can sometimes strut like a horse, if he wishes to do so'* (7).

In *Effort*, which he co-wrote with Lawrence, Laban comments that *'favourite habits of efforts are shown in all the everyday movements. Many of the movements seen during conversation, in leisure time, play and games, or even relaxation and rest, reveal much of the general effort make-up of a man.. Any small twitch of the face or hand might show habitual efforts.... Movement in industrial work is only one special case where human effort and its balance become observable. The nervous reactions in emotion and thinking produce many movements in which the effort-habits of a person are mirrored'*(8). He stated that *'Any bodily action can be understood as using one of the various combinations of the subdivisions of body, time, space and energy.'* He believed that describing them is *'thinking in terms of movement'*(9).

Efforts

All movements are alterations in the position of the body or part of the body in the space surrounding it. They take a certain time and demand a specific energy. There is a relationship between exertion and control.

Laban wrote:

'it is possible to determine and to describe any bodily action by answering four questions:

1 Which part of the body moves?

2 How much time does it require?

3 What degree of muscular energy is spent on the movement?

4 In which direction or directions of space is the movement exerted?'

He then suggests a way of defining a specific movement.

If it is:

1 The right leg

2 Quick

3   Strong

4   Forwards

Then it can be clearly defined as a *'thrusting kick of the leg in a forward direction'*(10).

The body can be divided into two major sections: above the point of levity in the trunk and below it, ie the point of leverage around the waist. Actions that take place motivated away from the pull of gravity, in the upper part of the body, are lighter in energy or weight than those in the lower part, which use a stronger weight as they give in to gravity. The time the movement takes can be sustained or quick; the directions in space can be direct or moving flexibly between points of space. The flow of these efforts can be executed with more or less tension; they can be free or bound.

Therefore, the motion factors are weight, space, time and flow.

Weight

Initially, this term relates to the relationship of gravity, up and away from it or giving in to it. It also refers to the amount of effort needed to operate on an object; the different strengths needed to lift something light or heavy. Certain groups and areas of muscular action are needed to lift something heavy or light. Try touching, gripping, lifting and carrying different objects, without worrying about any other factors, to experience which parts of the body are engaged.

Space

This refers to the fact that all our movements take place in the space around us. The desire to move is related to need. What can we learn about the particular direction the movement happens in?

Time

All movement happens over time. However, it is not only duration but also rhythm. Therefore, the best measurement is tempo, which carries within it the sense of being influenced by our own internal dynamics: heart, blood flow, breath. Is it in a quick tempo or a slower and sustained tempo?

Flow

Movements take place with a greater or lesser fluidity. What motivates that fluidity and what does it do to movement?

Weight, space, time and flow are subdivided again into their *elements* which indicate the gradations of intensity in executing them.

weight	strong	light
space	direct	flexible
time	quick	sustained
flow	bound	free

Laban suggested a link between personal efforts and personal character qualities. *'It is easy to perceive the aim of a person's movement if it is directed to some tangible object. Yet there also exist intangible values that inspire movement.'* (11)

Mental Efforts and Inner Participations

The four motion factors, weight, space, time and flow, could be linked to the four fundamental human temperaments, sensing, thinking, intuiting and feeling.

The motion factors have an internal connection that inspires their use. They are triggered by ways of going about doing something that the person wants to achieve. In different people certain elements will come into play more than others. The same objective can be achieved via all the elements;

they just take on different colours. So someone who wants to comfort you may have a 'bedside manner' or they may tell you to 'pull yourself together'. This will be experienced by the receiver as gentle or firm. Either method may seem forceful, physically manoeuvring the receiver into getting better. Or another person may try and move you more by standing back, reasoning or empathising; the ways are infinite and they all feel, sound and seem different, coming from different internal energies (*mental factors*) and different internal connections (*inner participations*).

Weight and Inner Participation

Weight is connected to the *inner participation* of *intending* – a strong or light desire to do something.

This is experienced in the *door plane*: stand with your feet planted, just over a shoulder-width apart, with your arms stretched out above your head so that your body forms an X (like standing inside a door frame; hence the name). This vertical plane with its sense of going down to the floor and up to the ceiling, with no reference to behind or in front, is the dimension of 'weight'. Try standing up with a firm intention to go somewhere and do something; this will have a strong energy; sit down again, slump forward then sit up and let the movement from the waist accompany a statement of intent. The statement will be lighter but it is still felt in the vertical plane. This is bringing weight into play.

Weight is experienced through the mental factor of sensing: knowing kinaesthetically just how much strength is needed to tackle a task.

It corresponds to: '*What* am I doing.'

Time and Inner Participation

Time is connected to the *inner participation* of *deciding* – decisions can be made quickly or over a sustained time period.

This is experienced in the *wheel plane*: move forward by reaching forward with your left leg, transfer your weight onto it, follow that reach with your arm and then propel yourself along that trajectory with wheel-like motions of your arms. Then try making a decision about something, not reflecting on it, just turning the possibilities over and over in your head; as you do this try walking backwards and forwards, try it slowly and then quickly. This feels like a physicalisation of the deciding process.

Time is experienced through the mental factor of intuiting: the kind of 'thinking' that is joining together things we already know, and can foresee, as apart from reflecting or coining thoughts anew.

It corresponds to: '*When* am I doing it.'

Flow and Inner Participation

Flow is connected to the *inner participation* of *adapting* – either freeing up or restricting the operation of the other motion factors.

It is experienced on the *table plane*: lie flat on the floor with arms and legs spread wide; that is the free flow on the table plane, a feeling of being completely open. Now stand up and try and recreate that openness of feeling trying to lean back as far as you can on an imaginary table hanging round your waist, and as far forward as you can and to both sides. Now imagine welcoming someone, flinging your arms open wide; that is free flow. Now welcome them with arms crossed; that is bound flow.

It is experienced through the mental factor of feeling: the emotional connection to what we are doing.

It corresponds to: '*How* am I doing it.'

Space and Inner Participation

Space is connected to the *inner participation* of *attending* – we can focus directly on something or let our attention be taken by something on a winding or flexible path like a figure of eight.

It is experienced as direct or flexible in diagonals of space. If you put the door plane, the wheel plane and the table plane together in a three-dimensional structure and filled in the space round them, you would have a cube. The dimensions of space are the lines that criss-cross this cube. Imagine yourself as the man in the circle in the square as in Leonardo da Vinci's drawing; now imagine that square is a cube. Stretch your right arm up to the right hand corner of the cube and then your left arm down behind you to the left hand bottom corner of the cube and imagine a line joining them through your body. Now look up towards your right hand and then let your thought travel down the line to where your left hand is pointing. This is one of the diagonals of space; it can travel, of course, way beyond the dimensions of the cube, but that is its direction. Repeat on the other side and continue playing with as many dimensions as possible. One of the other important factors is the ability to travel the arm across your body; the right hand can point towards the top left hand corner and so on; when it crosses your body it loses its freedom to be flexible.

Think of something that needs to be done; a small problem that you need to solve. Where does your head move, where do your eyes focus? Somewhere on a diagonal of space; think back to where the problem stemmed from, your eyes move along that diagonal back through your mind; now think about how this could have been dealt with or may be dealt with; the sensation is of thinking in curves and twists and wavy lines or figures of eight, somewhere in the space around you or in your head.

Space is experienced through the mental factor of thinking – focusing the attention.

It corresponds to '***Where*** am I doing it.'

Now try the 'comforting scenario', trying out each of the different motion factors in turn and isolating what internal changes are taking place; how different do they seem to you? Some may be easier to access than others because each person will show more or less inclination to the elements. Moreover, Laban describes how in *Weight* some may struggle against and some may indulge it; in *Time* there may be an absence or presence of rapidity; in *Space* some people evince a restriction to the extension and expansion of their movements, which appear to be as direct as possible; and in *Flow* some enjoy letting movements flow and others withhold or stop the flow. He calls this a 'struggle against' or 'indulgence in' the efforts concerned. Each person has a favoured method of engaging with each of the factors.

All the planes can be combined to form a cube. The cube is the construction inside which you can illustrate and experience the combinations of the motion factors that create the working actions.

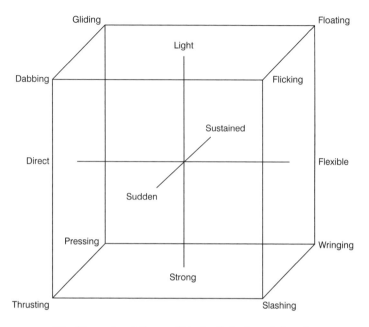

(The Dimensional Cross within the Cube from *Laban for all* by Jean Newlove & John Dalby)

Before you explore them try moving around in the dimensions of the cube from high to low, side to side, forward and back and along the diagonals; try it with across the body movements as well; try it with a gathering gesture or a scattering and reaching gesture.

Working Actions

No one person works off any one motion factor; there is always a combination. Observing and analysing someone is fundamental to movement analysis and these sequences can be practised and felt. They are called working actions because they echo the movements used in work. For instance, Laban wrote: '*The movements made in chopping wood consist of repeated hits, using the forearm. The same movements are made as the result of an inner excitement – of course without hatchet and wood – to signify a desire to hit out at the cause of the excitement, as one would hit out at an adversary.'* ie the basic actions of a working person are at the same time the *'fundamental movements of emotional and mental expression.'*(12)

The motion factors can be combined to create eight efforts or working actions.

strong	direct	quick	=	punching
strong	direct	sustained	=	pressing
strong	flexible	quick	=	slashing
strong	flexible	sustained	=	wringing
light	direct	quick	=	dabbing
light	direct	sustained	=	gliding
light	flexible	quick	=	flicking
light	flexible	sustained	=	floating

These are generic descriptions; it is up to the actor to choose a more specific verb to fit them, for instance, a 'punching' type of working action could be a kick or a thrust. They can also be experienced as a scattering or gathering action: pressing can be manifested in pushing away or drawing towards in a pressing manner.

This effort combination is the inner action.

'The richness of peoples' efforts consists just in the fact that their effort characteristics are an incredibly subtle mixture of many degrees of attitudes towards several motion factors.' As an extreme example, *'The 'indulger in' all the motion factors (i.e. yielding) will have a greater ability for delicate mental operations, while the 'fighter against' (i.e. contending) all the motion factors will be able to deal with mental work in which quick decision and accuracy are demanded.'*(13)

Try out the different combinations. Find a movement that seems to encapsulate each of the descriptions. Make sure that you find a figure of eight in the flexible movements; that is what distinguishes a wringing from a pressing action, for instance. Start with real objects and a real working action: wringing out a wet towel, for example, as apart from a lighter enfolding action to explore floating. Remember that the strong weight actions need to engage with the lower part of the trunk and the energies that transmit through the legs, giving in to gravity. Explore the difference between doing it with a free flowing ease or a more restricted bound flow.

Having located the different actions – and take time to do this – perform them again, but this time without the real object. Now ask yourself what provides the nature of the energy. It still needs to be the strength of the obstacle. Whatever was difficult in turning a tap caused that effort response; this now needs to be an abstract obstacle so that you still manufacture the same energy even though there is no *visible* reason.

Once you have located those energies ask yourself how you feel as you do each one. Then let a song come out of the energy. Some are potentially very obvious, some songs were created to accompany work effort, most notably slave songs or rowing songs. Try and find a song that comes out of the energies, not a song that describes how you feel as a result of the energies expended. Make sure that you fully explore each of the working actions and that you explore them in their gathering and scattering modes, in free and in bound flow. Note the difference each time.

Repeat the exercise but this time let a phrase come; the phrase must fill out effort movement.

In these exercises you may find that you favour one or other of the motion factors inside the combination. Maybe you can do sustained with ease when it is combined with light and flexible, but not when it is combined with strong and flexible. Try isolating which combinations are easiest for you. In order to transform energies to find other peoples' characteristics it is necessary to work on the combinations that are more difficult.

In all of these exercises it is important to focus on how it makes you feel, what it makes you think, what the obstacle may induce you to use in this particular combination of effort. Is it a change in obstacle that alters whether you use more of one motion factor than another in the effort? Does the change of obstacle make you use a different emphasis?

Having found a phrase that works as *strong*, *direct* and *sustained*, for instance, decide who you might be saying it to and why. Try it out and then keep the phrase but change the motivation and the person. Can you alter the emphasis? Do you find that you are still *strong*, *direct* and *sustained* and the phrase still makes sense, but that this time you would probably describe the sensation as *direct*, *strong* and *sustained* rather than *strong*, *direct* and *sustained*? It could be that this time the 'attending'/'thinking' factors are in the ascendant.

Do this in pairs, let one half of the group observe the differences. Once you have located a different balance of motion factors in the working actions see if the phrase needs to change slightly. Do the individual words need to have different qualities? Is the tempo and direction of the phrase more marked than the strength?

A very interesting music exercise was invented by Julian Dawes at Drama Centre to explore the sensation of the dynamics of the working actions. The student lies on the floor in a comfortable semi-supine posture and then starts to sing as banal a song as possible, something like 'happy birthday to you'. Then the workshop leader suggests an image such as 'bulldozer' and the student lets the image in and allows the singing to respond to the image. It is important not to hang on to the tune or its tempo. Then the leader suggests another image such as 'kangaroo' and so on through eight images that potentially encapsulate the working actions. The voice alters in tempo and weight very obviously and the listener can hear the altered shades and strength of the voice.

The conventional wisdom is that 'sticks and stones can break my bones but words can never hurt me'. If this is so, why do we feel 'warmed' by some people when they are 'nice' to us and 'bruised and battered' by others when we have been told off, for instance? Energies of language are key to our understanding of what people want from us.

Inner Attitudes and Incomplete Effort

When motion factors are combined they give a mode or *inner attitude*. They are also described as *incomplete efforts* because they are constantly moving between the factors, keeping the inner alive. Laban describes incomplete actions as being governed by which motion factors prevail or are absent in a sequence of movements. *'There can be in a picture that appears to be "mainly blue" traces of other colour; but some colours are definitely not there.'* So the movement-expressions of a person can thus be governed by one sort of action, when you would, for instance, say, *'(it) is mainly gliding although there are present suggestions of slashing, while punching or wringing actions might be absent.'* (14)

The inner attitude is observable in the *shadow moves* or *shadow actions*; these are the twitches, the gestures, the subliminal movements that indicate what the inner mode actually is. They show what the subjective relation to the obstacle is, even if the person is attempting in the outer to behave in ways that they objectively feel is appropriate to dealing with the obstacle. Laban analysis and use enables a very specific comprehension of inner attitudes and the relation of inner to outer. We signal very clearly 'where we are coming from' in the way we speak and, if we don't, then we will see i in the gestures that the body is making despite ourselves: the impatient twitching of the lips or tapping of the foot, despite saying 'take your time'; the crossed arms when we are trying to be open in our speech. This has now become a part of common observation in the term 'body language'.

Combinations that make up the inner attitude:

Weight + Space = Stable
Time and Flow are absent; there is a sense of constancy.

Weight + Time = Near
Space and Flow are absent; this mode operates in a narrow space and with an awareness of presence and decisions; an assurance.

Weight + Flow = A dream
Time and Space are absent; this mode is characterised by the lack of any thought or decision-making processes and is highly informed by the emotional/adaptive processes.

Space + Time = Awake
Weight and Flow are absent; there is an awareness and attention which is moderated by certainty or lack of certainty.

Space + Flow = Remote
Weight and time are absent; there is a sense of detachment, existing in the space dimensions moderated by the adapting/emotional factors. There is no sensual presence.

Flow + Time = Mobile
Weight and Space are absent; there is a constant movement and changeability.

Locating your own preferred mode and the working actions you favour enables you to begin the process of transformation. It aids the analysis of other characters and allows improvisation to occur from different centres of operation.

Externalised Drives

There is one further refinement which Laban was in the process of researching and that is *externalised drives*. These describe the combination of inner attitudes that activate the conscious actions, where the absence of one motion factor leads to a very pronounced sense of the behaviour.

Doing   has no adapting; it is intending/attending/deciding

Passion has no attending; it is intending/deciding/adapting

Vision   has no intending; it is attending/deciding/adapting

Spell   has no deciding; it is intending/attending/adapting

Spell is probably the easiest one to grasp because of the idea of spellbinding, which carries in it a sense of timelessness, filling our senses, our feelings and our space. *Vision*, in common thought, often implies an inability to do anything practical whereas someone who is a *doing* person could easily be visualised as someone who has no room for emotional intervention. Similarly the idea of someone involved in *passion* who does not use or who loses their head is an easy image to grasp. These are not only motivating forces but visible in their movement manifestation.

Application

Applying Laban's movement work opens up the movement imagination and enables the precise notation of mime and dance improvisations. However, this chapter is focusing on how to apply his work to acting improvisation and text.

Essentially, Laban has given us the tools for analysis of character and characteristics and tools for transformation, a means whereby we can move out of our comfort zone and try to move ourselves towards a character.

The following exercises play with finding different operational *centres*. They are not Laban exercises per se, or as described in any of the literature, but they are ways of enabling the student to sense and feel the effect of his explorations. They may also aid the understanding of how to apply them to character and text work. At each stage the student should be taken back to the *neutral experience*, which will help them to find the way in which the body connects in free flow.

For the *neutral experience*, imagine that a string with a weight attached is held by the centre of the ear. It would create a straight line over the shoulder, hip and ankle, putting the body onto its centre from which any movement is easily available and creating an optimum state of readiness and awareness. There is no imposition of any attitude or feeling. This can be tested by dropping onto one hip and seeing how that feels, then the other and seeing how that feels. Experiment with leaning slightly forward, slightly back, too stretched upwards, and too slumped. These will make the student aware of how the slightest movement influences how they feel. Neutral is when none of that comes into play.

Laban believed that the whole body needed to be working harmoniously in order for the voice to function.

Observation Work

Play 'follow my leader' in pairs; observe how different the weight distribution is with each person. The 'leader' drops out and the follower keeps the walk going, seeing how it feels, how the different energies affect them. Is there a different speed? Is there a lighter or stronger energy? Does the person have a fixed focus or a more flexible focus? Change over so that the follower now leads and repeat.

Now think of someone who is very different from you that you know well. Try and imagine that person in front of you – a ghostly leader – and follow them round the room, slowly getting a sense of how they are moving and behaving; at a given moment allow the 'ghost' to stop and then walk through them picking up their qualities, like a coat, as you go on. Continue walking around as that person; stop, start, sit down, look out of the window and do any other daily actions that you think of. Then find something to do physically (like sorting out your bag) or something else that might be more specific to that person (like cleaning the room). Then take yourself out and talk to other members of the group; find something you need from them like directions to somewhere. Find out how you ask and give directions, whether your voice has different qualities or whether your sentence structure is different. Do people behave differently to you in that mode than they normally do?

Once you have stopped, assess in what way it felt different. What habits or gestures did you discover? What changes did you notice? How did you behave? The exercise can be repeated again. It might be good to have half the group observe the other half so that they can feed back the differences they observed.

This exercise overlaps with a Stanislavski exercise of self-endowment, treating yourself as if you are someone else, which is a very useful way of getting to grips with a character you don't understand. You think 'this person is very like x' and then try a rehearsal in the self endowment of x.

Hopefully the student will have discovered that they think or feel differently inside the ghost skin. Now begin to explore those differences further. Start by exploring neutral (see above). Close your eyes and the body will slowly rock and circle to its neutral position; keep the knees relaxed. From that position, start to move away from your spot. Do it again and see if you are aware of where you are motivating your movement from. Let the group watch each individual move from 'neutral' and see if they can observe the trigger. Does one person perhaps drop their eyes just before they move? Does another seem to flick out with the knee or the foot? Does it tally with the sensation of following them in the previous exercise? How would you describe each persons' movement? Can you fit it into one of the generic working actions?

Now move around the room as you would normally; just think of how you are feeling and where you might be going. Now imaginatively focus your mind and think that you are leading from your heart. Make sure it's not your chest, but your heart; don't stick your chest out or distort your body, don't 'do' leading from the heart, just think that your heart leads you. Discover how that makes you feel. Does it change your sense of where you are going and what you are doing or your attitude? Let a song come to you. Stop singing and then let a piece of text come to you. Say it out loud over and over again as you move around. Now find an object and start to work with it as before (tidying your belongings, or cleaning the room). Now write something, a letter to a friend perhaps, or maybe you find you want to write a more important letter.

This exercise can be repeated for as many different 'centres' as you want. Try below the waist (backs of the thighs, feet) as well as above. Try nose, eyes, ears; try behind as well as in front. Sometimes the response to the 'centres' shows that we have many words and phrases in English to describe the feeling of being in a specific centre of operation. But feeling gutsy or hearty is different from greedy or loving, for instance, even if the initial area of focus may be identical (the gut or the heart). Each 'centre' causes different sensations. It also triggers different combinations. Again one student may discover that the 'lighter' energies seem to trigger quick energies and the stronger ones 'sustained' energies and another may find entirely the opposite. This helps you find which combinations are harder for you. You discover this in the songs that occur or the bits of text you find yourself saying. Different desires seem to emerge from different 'centres'. In the process of working with the different objects, did the student find that they related differently to objects depending on the energy focus they were using? Did they use language differently? Did they touch thoughts and ideas they don't normally find?

Think of the one that was very different from you and the more difficult one. Repeat the process and then write a diary entry for the day you have had (as the character). Then write a monologue of about two minutes length. Make sure there is a reason for the character to talk; they should want something of importance, rather like Alan Bennett's *Talking Heads*. Rehearse it at home and then at the next session perform it for the group. Ask the group what kind of working actions they perceived; what kind of inner attitude they think the character has.

Text

Differing sentence structures and types of words will provide clues to different types of characters and shadow moves. Laban noted that the movement of the speech organs that form sound, and therefore words, was the same as any other muscular movement.

Find a short piece of text. Feel the shapes of the words and sentences, to the full stop, not just the phrase. What kind of energy is in the words? What kind of working action do you find? Think of a doing word, a transitive verb that fits the working action, then that is what the character is saying it for to do that to the other person (to excite them, to taunt them and so on). This is what would be called an activity, action or tactic in Stanislavski-type analyses; it is what is referred to as 'actioning' the text. If you find lots of repeated behaviour which just has shades of variation, such as prick, poke, goad then that starts to give you clues as to the inner attitude and drive of the character.

Another way to find the dynamic is to dance the text; move it inside the cube; find out if it's flexible or direct. If it has lots of commas then it is likely to be flexible as it is hard to be direct while weaving your way round commas. Do the words have light or strong qualities, are they 'airy' or 'sensuous'? What does the energy used tell you about the nature of the obstacle, the problem that is making the character use that kind of dynamic? Is the obstacle apparent or not, internal or external? If someone seems to be 'using a hammer to crack a nut' then it is possible that the obstacle is internal as well as external.

This work enables you to explore inner and outer at the same time. It allows you to feel through the text in order to locate and name it, giving you a sense of the basic mode of operation of the character, rather than only allowing an academic analysis. It also gives you a firm basis from which to improvise the character and an assured way of reading the text kinaesthetically.

Laban's work in understanding the nature and expression of movement has provided a wonderful base for exploring the energy and dynamic of language as well as the impulse to speak.

DISCUSSION POINTS

- In what way were Laban's ideas different from movement as physical exercise?

- Why do Laban's concepts work for both dancers and actors?

- Laban said that the basic actions of a working person are also the movements of emotional and mental expression. What does he mean?

- How do the motion factors and mental factors interact?

- Think of a character from a film or a play you've seen or studied, and describe their inner attitudes and working actions.

- How would you describe your own physical habits, habitual efforts and gestures? Which of these do you find the most difficult to change?

- How would you explore a character's working actions as part of a rehearsal process?

Bibliography and Further Reading

Laban, R. – *The Mastery of Movement for the Stage.* Macdonald & Evans, 1950

Laban, R. & Lawrence, F.C. – *Effort (Economy of Human Movement).* Macdonald & Evans, 1947

Newlove, J. – *Laban for Actors and Dancers.* Nick Hern Books, 1993

Newlove, J. & Dalby, J. – *Laban for All.* Nick Hern Books, 2004

Hodgson, J. & Preston-Dunlop, V. – *Rudolf Laban: An Introduction to his Work and Influence.* Northcote House, 1990

Partsch-Bergsohn, I. & Bergsohn, H. – *The Makers of Modern Dance in Germany.* Princeton Book Company, 2003

Wilk, C. (ed.) – *Modernism 1914-1939 Designing a New World.* V&A Publications, 2006

Notes and References

(1) Wilk, C. (ed.) – *Modernism 1914-1939 Designing a New World.* V&A Publications, 2006

(2) *Ibid*

(3) Bergsohn and Bergsohn – *The Makers of Modern Dance in Germany.* Princeton Book Company, 2003. Quote taken from *A Life in Dance* by Rudolf Laban Macdonald and Evans, 1948

(4) Laban, R. – *The Mastery of Movement for the Stage.* Macdonald & Evans, 1950

(5) *Ibid*

(6) *Ibid*

(7) *Ibid*

(8) Laban, R. & Lawrence, F.C. – *Effort (Economy of Human Movement).* Macdonald & Evans, 1947

(9) Laban, R. – *The Mastery of Movement for the Stage.* Macdonald & Evans, 1950

(10) *Ibid*

(11) *Ibid*

(12) *Ibid*

(13) Laban, R. & Lawrence, F.C. – *Effort (Economy of Human Movement).* Macdonald & Evans, 1947

(14) Laban, R. – *The Mastery of Movement for the Stage.* Macdonald & Evans, 1950

Chapter Three

Acting Brecht

by

Stephen Unwin

A Word of Warning

Bertolt Brecht (1898-1956) is one of the most influential figures of 20th Century theatre. He was both a remarkable dramatist who wrote a dozen landmark plays and an astonishing director who devised a radical new approach to the theatre.

Brecht has an unjustified, if understandable, reputation for Germanic seriousness, and his writings on the theatre present the actor with a series of terms which can, at first, seem bewildering. He once joked that 'a man with one theory is lost. He must have several, four, many!' and it is impossible to describe his approach to the theatre without revealing numerous inconsistencies and contradictions. In exploring the subject, it's worth bearing in mind four key points:

1   Brecht's theories cannot be understood without some grasp of the circumstances in which he lived. Faced with the multiple disasters of German history – defeat in World War I, the economic crisis of the 1920s and '30s, the rise of Hitler, the catastrophe of World War II and the divided country that followed – Brecht wanted the theatre to help build a better future. Paraphrasing Karl Marx, he declared that 'the artists have hitherto interpreted the world, the point is to change it', and everything he did sprang from this imperative.

2   Much of Brecht's most important theoretical work was written in exile, first in Scandinavia and then in the United States. In neither place could he stage his plays or work as a director, and the writing of these essays became a substitute for productions. It was only after his return to Germany in 1948 that he could put his ideas into practice.

3   It is sometimes assumed that as a Marxist, Brecht's working class characters must be heroes. In fact, the opposite is usually the case: Brecht was fascinated by why the poor so often fail to act in their own best interests and are humiliated and destroyed as a result. He was a realistic writer who wanted to show the truth, not propaganda, and it is important not to confuse his commitment to artistic simplicity with simplistic content.

4   Brecht was concerned above all to engage his actors – and, more importantly, his audiences – with the realities of the world and he constantly joked, mocked, provoked and cajoled to get his point across. He was an enormous personality – brash but wise, serious and ironic, intellectual as well as flippant – and it's a mistake to read his theory without some sense of his tone of voice. When asked by a group of eager young English actors whether their production of *Life of Galileo* had produced the famous 'alienation effect', Helene Weigel, Brecht's wife and great exponent of his work, replied: 'Oh, that was just a silly phrase Bert came up with to stop his actors from over-acting'. Brecht wasn't interested in creating a science for acting; if anything he wanted acting to be about something more important than acting.

The Evolution of Brecht's Theatre

Brecht was suspicious of all claims to eternal truth and a survey of his approach to acting needs to place his theories within the context of a changing world, as well as his own development as playwright and director.

From Expressionism to the New Objectivity

Defeat in World War I (1914-18) was a catastrophe for Germany. The failure of the German Communist Revolution and the draconian terms of the Treaty of Versailles (both 1919) radicalised opinion and stored up trouble for the future. The dominant artistic form was Expressionism: a rejection of the objectivity of both Impressionism and Naturalism and an attempt to express widespread feelings of worry and despair.

Brecht's relationship to Expressionism was complex. His first three plays – *Baal* (1918), *Drums in the Night* (1920) and *In the Jungle of the Cities* (1924) – all have expressionist features (fragmentary poetry, disconnected story-telling and minimal psychological realism) and actors in these plays need to display often inchoate feelings of pain and anxiety. But they also have a quality which was quite novel at the time: they are edgy and ironic and for the most part do not require the emotional torrents demanded by Expressionism. What's more, unlike much Expressionist drama, they are interested in the underdog, the outcast and the villain.

From the outset it was clear that Brecht's plays needed a new kind of acting and he directed a number of radical and explosive productions in the 1920s, mostly of his own plays, in order to find out what that might be. He wanted a kind of theatre that was both objective and analytical, popular and theatrical. The climax was his 1931 production of *Man Equals Man* (1924-26), which shows an ordinary man being 'reassembled like a car' and turned into a 'human fighting machine'. It is a deconstruction of the very idea of the individual and presents the Stanislavskian-trained actor with a profound challenge. Brecht did away with all attempts at psychological truth, and created an astonishing montage. The Russian playwright Sergei Tretiakov described it in vivid terms:

'Giant soldiers armed to the teeth and wearing jackets caked with lime, blood and excrement stalk about the stage, holding on to wires to keep them from falling off the stilts inside their trouser legs.' [1]

Inspired by the pioneering directorial work of Erwin Piscator, as well as the theatrical experiments of early Soviet theatre, Brecht's revolutionary approach borrowed from a wide range of popular entertainments: the circus, fairgrounds, sport (particularly boxing) and even the military. These, he argued, provided useful models for a theatre which could communicate the tough realities of a dog-eat-dog world and articulate his central point: that character is formed by environment and that the human subject is a product of the world in which he lives.

Music Theatre and Kurt Weill

The late 1920s were the golden age of the Weimar Republic and for five or six years Germany saw a startling new acceptance of self-expression, individual sexuality and women's rights. Fusing the popular with the avant-garde, the satirical with the passionate and the pleasurable with the savage, a large number of remarkable poets, painters, musicians and entertainers made Berlin the centre of a unique flowering of the creative arts.

In 1927, Brecht met the composer Kurt Weill. Together they wrote *The Threepenny Opera* (1928), perhaps the definitive work of Weimar culture. It has very little to say about crime – or indeed its causes – but instead consists of a vivid patchwork of pastiche, irony and quoted sentimentality. Again, actors approaching this material need to accept that Stanislavskian investigation into characters is futile: there is very little psychology in Mac the Knife, Polly Peachum and the rest. Brecht wanted something much more immediate – an almost anarchistic theatrical energy which confronts the audience even as it confuses them, which stirs them up even as it entertains them. Actors need to bring, above all, a strong streak of satirical wit – as well as a readiness to accept that the characterisation is provisional and sketchy.

A significant feature of *The Threepenny Opera* is the way that Brecht and Weill insisted that their roughly hewn songs should be separated from the scenes in which they appear. This, of course, has its roots in classical opera, with its clearly defined arias, trios, ensembles etc, but Brecht required something unique: that the performers shouldn't slide from the spoken text into the song and that the songs should be sung as separate numbers, often directly to the audience, with their own lighting. Brecht wanted his audience to listen to each song on its own terms and by dividing them into discrete elements he ensured that they would.

A Marxist Theatre

The Weimar Republic came to a dramatic end with the Wall Street Crash of October 1929: Germany was soon plunged into a profound economic depresssion which caused rapid political polarisation and the exponential growth of both Communist and Fascist parties – most ominously, of course, Hitler's National Socialists. These tensions overflowed onto the streets of the big cities, often with shocking brutality.

The most significant artistic response was the 'New Objectivity'. This movement rejected the excesses of Expressionism and strove instead for artistic modernity inspired by the straight lines of the American city, the crisp democratic energy of the sporting arena and the clarity and ideals of the machine age. The most remarkable results were in architecture and design (particularly at the Bauhaus), but also influenced film, music, fine art and the theatre.

Brecht developed a new kind of drama, the *Lehrstück*. There are half a dozen of these: the masterpieces are *The Mother* (1930) and *The Decision* (1931). Written to b performed by a mixture of politically committed professionals and amateurs – *'those people who neither can pay for art nor are paid for art, but just want to take part in it'*(2), as Brecht wrote – these short 'learning plays' were designed, above all, to teach political tactics to Communist Party activists.

Formally, the *Lehrstücke* borrowed from a range of sources: the theatrical simplicity of oriental drama, the technological modernity of the radio play and the austere grandeur of Bach's choral works. They use music extensively, by all four of Brecht's musical collaborators – Paul Dessau, Kurt Weill, Hanns Eisler and Paul Hindemith – and can be remarkably powerful when performed with their original scores. They make their points, which can be difficult to grasp, with the utmost simplicity and theatrical elegance.

The *Lehrstücke* do not present actors with any huge challenges: the action must be vivid, the words of the songs and the choruses need to be clearly enunciated and the verse should be addressed directly to the audience. Most importantly, actors need to be absolutely clear about the purpose of each scene, and the point of the piece as a whole. Brecht positively discouraged a Stanislavskian approach and prevented the actors from identifying with their characters, even insisting that the Young Comrade in *The Decision* – who is shot because he endangers the cause – should be played by all four performers in turn.

Political Naturalism

In January 1933, Hitler became Chancellor of Germany and quickly assumed dictatorial powers; Brecht fled soon after, for his own safety. After a short stay in France, he settled with his wife and two children in Denmark – and then in Sweden and Finland – close enough to Germany to return if the political situation improved. There he wrote several volumes of astonishing poetry, some of his most important plays, and developed many of his ideas for a new kind of theatre which could reflect on what he called the 'dark times'.

Responding to the call for artists on the left to produce popular, accessible work that could mobilise support for the broad struggle against fascism, not just in Germany but throughout Europe, Brecht wrote two important naturalist works: the one act play set in the Spanish Civil War, *Señora Carrara's Rifles* (1937) (adapted from J.M. Synge's *Riders to the Sea*) and the great cycle of short plays about everyday life in the early years of Hitler's rule, *Fear and Misery of the Third Reich* (1935-38).

These plays, though highly sophisticated, were designed to be performed by amateurs. They mark the fundamental transition to Brecht's mature style and acting them requires both attention to naturalistic detail and an acute sense of the political point behind each dramatic moment.

Epic Realism

Brecht left Scandinavia for Hollywood in 1941 and tried to make it as a writer of film scripts. Although he struggled in America, it was in exile that he wrote his five masterpieces: *Mother Courage and Her Children* (1939), *The Good Person of Szechwan* (1939-41), *Life of Galileo* (1938-39, 1945-47), *Puntila and his Man Matti* (1940) and his most popular work *The Caucasian Chalk Circle* (1943-45). These draw together all the various strands of Brecht's work and fuse them into a new kind of theatre, perhaps best called epic realism.

By his own admission, Brecht stole an enormous amount from Shakespeare and acting in these plays requires many of the same skills that Shakespeare does: closely observed human realism combined with a clear sense of what is being shown; sophisticated historical insight and biting contemporary satire; a sense of epic scale but precise domestic detail; a careful presentation of the material facts of the characters' lives and considerable theatrical chutzpah. And, in Brecht, all this needs to be driven by a commitment to sharing his understanding of the world with the audience.

Brecht was fascinated by contradiction. it is in contradictions that we best understand the impact of society on the individual. Thus, Mother Courage is spirited and remarkable, but also greedy and blind; Galileo is heroic in his pursuit of pure science, but compromised by the deal he makes with the Inquisition; Shen Teh is a kind prostitute who wants to do good, but Shui-Ta, her male alter-ego, is a vicious exploiter. The conscious presentation of these many contradictions lie at the heart of Brecht's approach and must on no account be glossed over or downplayed.

It was also in exile, cut off from his audience and his theatre, that Brecht developed the main themes of his approach to the theatre, and described them in a number of theoretical essays: the most important are *The Messingkauf Dialogues* (1940) and *The Short Organum for the Theatre* (1948).

The Berliner Ensemble

The defeat of Nazi Germany led to the division of Germany into two nations, one dominated by the Soviet Union, the other by the Western Powers. Brecht returned to East Germany in 1948 and was able to put his ideas into practice with the Berliner Ensemble, the company he founded with Helene Weigel, his wife and a great actress in her own right. There he directed a number of his greatest plays, including *Mother Courage* and *The Caucasian Chalk Circle*. If, as Brecht liked to say, 'the proof of the pudding is in the eating', then these astonishing productions demonstrated the real meaning of his theory. They are well documented in the 'Model Books': invaluable collections of notes and photographs intended, above all, to show what needs to be considered in staging one of the plays.

Acting Brecht

Brecht's theories throw up certain key phrases, the following pages try to clarify the most important ones and provide some examples of how they can be useful to the actor.

Status, Class and Money

As a Marxist, Brecht argued that society was disfigured by the gap between the rich and the poor, the powerful and the weak, the comfortable and the wretched, and everything he wrote was aimed at understanding the reasons for these inequalities and suggesting how they could be redressed.

Thus, in tackling a part in a Brecht play – or approaching other material in a Brechtian fashion – it is essential that the actor asks fundamental questions: what is his character's position in society? What does he do for a living? How much is he paid? How powerful is he? Who has control over him? And so on. The Stanislavskian actor tends to regard these questions as secondary; for Brecht they're the most important you can ask. Class, status and money are dominant forces in the formation of character and the actor needs to attend to the implications of this information.

It is essential that actors approach this subject with precision and do not generalise. They need to be particularly careful with working-class characters, a category which includes a wide range of different socio-economic groups peasants, industrial labourers, beggars, domestic workers and the unemployed. When talking about acting peasants, Brecht insisted that his actors should not try to play an abstract notion of 'the peasant'; instead, they should present a range of very different peasants – this one religious, that one greedy, this one timid, that one bold – allowing the audience to understand the class of the peasantry by seeing what binds these individuals together.

Most challenging of all, Brecht wanted his actors to show the way that changes in a character's economic status affect the way that he behaves. The transformation of Galy Gay in *Man Equals Man* is brought about through financial bribery as much as anything else and although by the end of the play Mother Courage is almost destitute, at other times she achieves a level of financial security and is almost middle-class: at her richest she celebrates the war that will destroy her.

There are many different ways of showing the impact of status, class and money – costumes, accents, moves, attitudes and so on – but these need to be executed with great precision and social insight. In paying for her daughter's funeral, Helene Weigel as Mother Courage put several coins in the peasant's hand and then took one back: at the emotional climax of the play she showed that Courage was still haggling, trying to preserve what little capital she had left.

The Alienation Effect

Brecht wanted to create a kind of theatre which would encourage his audience to look at what was being presented in such a way that they would think about their own lives and the society in which they lived and decide to change it. In 1940 he wrote:

> '*So the question is this: is it quite impossible to make the reproduction of real-life events the purpose of art and thereby make something conducive of the spectators' critical attitude toward them?* '(3)

The answer was the 'alienation effect' (*Verfremdungseffekt*, sometimes translated as 'estrangement'), one of the most misunderstood terms in the Brechtian vocabulary.

The 'alienation effect' requires the actor to *show* his character – not simply identify with him. The danger with identification, with submerging yourself in the character,

Brecht argued, was that it prevents a performance from having an active purpose; worse, it stops the audience from thinking about the action that is being presented.

To this end, Brecht asked his actors to tell their character's story with as much objectivity as possible. Just as witnesses of a car crash or a football match might describe what they had seen, drawing attention to the decisive moments, asking the listeners to look at what happened from a variety of perspectives, helping them come to their own judgment, so actors should approach their performance with a keen eye on what needs to be shown. Thus, Brecht would insist that actors in rehearsal perform in the third person, prefacing each speech with 'he said... she said...'. At other times, he asked them to highlight particularly important moments by adding 'instead of responding like this, he responded like that'. Such exercises help the actors discover what it is that the audience must see and understand.

Brecht wanted his actors to ensure that what is presented has quotation marks around it: 'this is what happened', 'this is who got hurt', 'this is who paid for the war'. He insisted that the actors should tell the story in such a way that the individual elements can be seen as temporary and subject to change – a long way from the notion of a theatre that offers its audience 'eternal truths'. And to this end he asked them to be involved in the practical presentation of the play – resetting props and scenery, putting on new costumes, etc. – in full view of the audience.

The phrase 'alienation effect' has sometimes led people to imagine that Brecht sought something that was cold or unenjoyable to watch. This, however, is a travesty: he wanted to prevent acting which failed to present the world realistically. Thus an actor playing Macbeth or Richard III shouldn't simply aim for the audience's sympathy at the great man's downfall; he should also show the steps that took him to power and the murderous deeds – and numerous victims – that defined his tyranny. This should be done with passion and power, but also with clarity and objectivity.

The 'alienation effect' is hardly novel. Brecht took it from a vast range of sources – Shakespeare, Oriental theatre, popular culture and so on – but forged it into a new acting style appropriate for the horrors and struggles of the 20th Century. His own summary can be found in a *Short Description of a New Technique of Acting which Produces an Alienation Effect* and at greater length in paragraphs 43–54 of *A Short Organum for the Theatre*.

Gestus

Another difficult term is *gestus*. At its most superficial, this is close to the English word 'gesture': the pointed finger, the shrugged shoulder, the turned back and so on. However, *gestus* also refers to something deeper: the physical embodiment of the relationships between people in society. Each *gestus* captures a particular set of interlocking attitudes and the sum total of these provides the audience with a chart of the society that is portrayed.

Understanding the *gestus* of any individual moment is an essential task in directing or acting in one of Brecht's plays. Thus, the way that Galileo teaches Andrea about the orbit of the earth around the sun has a different *gestus* from that shown when Galileo pretends that the telescope he presents to the Doge is his own invention. Similarly, the way that Mother Courage, all alone at the end, hauls the cart around the stage for the last time, still looking for business, is a unique and troubling *gestus*. A poor production would make it as pathetic as possible; Brecht's famous 1948 production showed a woman determined to continue living off the war, even though it had robbed her of everything.

Acting with *gestus* requires above all an understanding of the play and a desire to share that understanding with the audience. Brecht sometimes asked his actors in rehearsal to preface each action with a little comment: 'this is how the landlord pays his peasants wages', 'let me show you how the able-bodied beggar takes on the pose of a wounded war hero', 'look how Mother Courage defends her stock from demands for charity' and so on. Each of these observations should then be translated into a simple physical attitude, which can be readily understood by the viewer.

Telling the Story

Brecht emphasised the importance of plot: *'Everything'*, he wrote, *'hangs on the "story"; it is the heart of the theatrical performance'* (4) and it is interesting to see from his working notes just how central story outlines were to his writing: much of his preparation consisted of pure plot elements, free of opinion, character or meaning. He knew that the audience wants to find out what happens next and his best plays are rich with dramatic tension: Will Galileo repent in the face of the Inquisition? Will Grusha cross the bridge before the Ironshirts reach her? Will Kattrin succeed in saving the city of Halle?

But here there is an apparent contradiction: Brecht's plays often tell the audience the outcome in advance. This encourages them not simply to be gripped by the story, but to look at the particular way the outcome is reached: the effect is like a slow motion action replay, which lets us see the specific mistake that let in a goal; or an eyewitness report on a traffic accident. Again, this has ancient roots: classical myths, the Bible, *Romeo and Juliet*, all tell stories whose end we have already been told; it's how the end is reached which is interesting.

Brecht was eager to distinguish between traditional dramatic story-telling – 'this happens because that happened

– and the epic style – 'this happens and then that happens'. His plays are built out of discrete, dynamic units of action, which do not flow from one into the other, but jostle up against each other, like the separate episodes in an epic. This distinction is described in *The Modern Theatre is the Epic Theatre*.

The emphasis on dramatic action (as opposed to psychological introspection) deliberately avoids interpretation: it is the presentation of 'unvarnished raw material' that allows the audience to come to its own conclusions and see how the individual's actions are the direct result of the world in which he lives.

Dramatic story-telling shows that the world is subject to change and articulating that process of change and development – of history itself – is essential in the Brechtian theatre. Everything that takes place on stage should serve the story and the actor needs to keep the narrative in mind at all times: 'this is what happened', his performance seems to say, 'would it were otherwise'.

Direct Address

The term 'direct address' describes the moment when an actor steps out of the action and talks directly to the audience – usually in character, but sometimes as the actor himself – recognising that they are present and ignoring the naturalistic convention of the 'fourth wall'.

In Brecht, direct address is used in a variety of ways: sometimes for straightforward narration (such as the Singer in *The Caucasian Chalk Circle*); at other times, characters talk to the audience in the first person 'confessional' mode (such as Wang in *The Good Person of Szechwan*). It is also used to provoke a particular understanding of the play (as in the verse of *The Decision* or *The Mother*). It is a mistake, however, to imagine that direct address is always solemn or didactic. In fact, the effect is often comic, giving the audience an opportunity to step back from the drama and look at what is being presented in a fresh way, enjoying a new perspective and looking at the drama with greater critical objectivity.

Caricatures of Brecht's theatre sometimes cite the use of direct address as an odd and somewhat sterile innovation; the fact that it is fundamental to much pre-Romantic and Shakespearean theatre is usually forgotten.

Playing Things Historically

Brecht knew that it was impossible to create a new kind of drama for the modern world without a profound feeling for history and acting in his plays requires a grasp not only of the circumstances in which he lived, but also of his own reading of the past. This had at its heart Hegel's theory of the dialectical processes of history, in which the conflict between classes and groups leads inexorably – and often bloodily – to a better society. This does not preclude the tragic, but places individual experience within a broader context of historical development.

Brecht's notion of 'playing things historically' means that the actors show that the behaviour and beliefs of the individual are created by the particular circumstances that surround him. Such an emphasis means that all notions of 'eternal truth' and 'human nature' should be replaced with an analysis of behaviour which is specific to social circumstances and changes according to historical context. A performance that does not take into account the historical forces that shape character cannot be convincing – not just in Brecht, many would say.

Brecht was particularly interested in discovering those places in the drama – the 'useful junction points', as he called them – where the clash between two periods and two belief systems is most evident: the feudal and the Renaissance in *Life of Galileo*, or the bourgeois and the revolutionary in *The*

Mother. Of course, such analysis runs the danger of over-simplification, but highlighting these moments encourages the audience to see the drama historically and helps them place individual actions within a broader context, as part of a continuous process of change.

Epic Theatre

Brecht's work deliberately eschews the sense of inevitability which is such a feature of 19th Century drama. Instead, he took inspiration for his notion of the 'epic theatre' from Shakespeare, whose plays are built out of a series of self-contained episodes and jump from location to location, unconfined by the Aristotelian unities of time and place. The epic style is evident wherever art deliberately pastes together conflicting elements, be it the Elizabethan theatre, popular culture, photo-montage or Dadaism: Brecht's great achievement was to borrow from everywhere and develop a theatrical technique of his own. Only the epic theatre, he argued, could express the bewildering disjointedness of modern life.

The essential point of the epic theatre is that stories are told through a collage of contrasting scenes whose content, style and approach are deliberately incongruous. A new artistic unity is built from this collection of disparate ingredients: interruptions are encouraged, text is set against action, music is given its own reality, scenery is cut away, unconnected scenes follow on from each other and so on. The point is that by exposing the viewers to such diversity of content and form, they are encouraged to think independently and come to their own conclusions. The epic theatre is nothing less than dialectics in practice.

Actors in the epic theatre should see the play as a collection of incidents which demonstrate different aspects of character according to changing circumstances. They need to relish the contradictions that this technique reveals and not attempt to smooth out the differences. An example might be Yvette, the prostitute in *Mother Courage*. When we first meet her, business is bad because all her customers know that she is riddled with venereal disease. The arrival of the Catholic army changes her situation dramatically (new clients who don't know her); but it is when she has become a rich woman that the transformation is the most extreme: the audience knows that she is still Yvette, but the actress needs to show just how different she is – wealthy, fat and powerful. As usual in Brecht, circumstances create personality, not the other way round.

Brecht tried to define the epic theatre on many occasions. Perhaps the most complete account can be found in *The Street Scene (A Basic Model for an Epic Theatre)*, *The Messingkauf Dialogues* and *A Short Organum for the Theatre*. Walter Benjamin's *What is Epic Theatre?* in *Understanding Brecht* is exceptionally revealing.

Playing One Thing After Another

A common criticism of Brecht's plays is that they are long-winded and boring. Certainly the larger ones benefit from judicious cutting and even the finest can, at times, seem over-extended.

One reason for this is Brecht's emphasis on 'playing one thing after another'. This means, primarily, a way of acting which allows the individual moments to be played for all their worth, giving the audience the space to look at each element separately, instead of being swept along uncritically by the action. Such productions tend to find detail in small social 'gests', whose inclusion illuminates the way that the society operates. These details – paying the servants, bowing to royalty etc – should not be glossed over, but can slow down the dramatic action. This all needs to be worked out and

Brecht's rehearsals were famously meticulous: each moment of action looked at from every conceivable perspective, and endlessly honed and refined.

However, in his finest work (*The Decision*, *The Mother*, *Life of Galileo*, *Mother Courage* and *The Caucasian Chalk Circle*) Brecht achieved an extreme economy of means – stripped of rhetoric, dramatically taut, simple and elegant – and they are at their best when played fast. One of the last things Brecht wrote was a note to the actors of the Berliner Ensemble on their first visit to London in August 1956:

> 'The English have long dreaded German art as sure to be dreadfully ponderous, slow, involved and pedestrian... So our playing must be quick, light and strong. By quickness I don't mean a frantic rush: playing quickly is not enough, we must think quickly as well. We must keep the pace of our run-throughs, but enriched with a gentle strength and our own enjoyment. The speeches should not be offered hesitantly, as though offering one's last pair of boots, but must be batted back and forth like ping-pong balls.' (5)

It should be pinned up in the rehearsal room of anyone attempting to stage Brecht today.

Contradictions

The key to drama lies in the conflict of opposites: one group wants one thing, another wants the opposite and the contention between the two resolves itself in a third position. Brecht felt that identifying such contradictions was an essential part of the theatre's role.

In his early work this is expressed in an insistent clash of registers: the sentimental followed by the cynical, the intellectual followed by the sensual, for example. The effect is to relativise any argument that is pursued and to undermine any feeling expressed. If the result was negative, it cleared the way for Brecht's understanding of the way that the contradictions inherent in society manifest themselves within the individual.

In his mature work, however, this interest became more positive, and his reading of Voltaire and classical Chinese philosophy made it into an exercise in clear thinking. 'On the one hand this, on the other hand that' was, he felt, the approach that stood most chance of approximating to the truth of the world. Apparently, while directing *The Caucasian Chalk Circle* with the Berliner Ensemble, Brecht exasperated his colleagues by continually exposing the contradictions implicit in every decision – including his own – and challenging them accordingly.

All of Brecht's greatest characters are constructed on contradictory principles: the 'good woman', Shen Teh, has to become the bad man, Shui Ta, in order to survive; Mother Courage sacrifices her children to the war in order to make a living; Galileo abandons pure scientific pursuit for the greater good because of its personal implications; and Puntila, who is generous when drunk, reverts to brutality when sober. The point is that these many contradictions are not the result of poor characterisation – they are deliberate and realistic portraits of the way real people behave in a contradictory world and actors should go out of their way to show up the nature of these contradictions.

Complex Seeing

As his political analysis matured, Brecht became increasingly interested in encouraging what he called 'complex seeing'. By this, he meant something more dynamic than mere despair at the myriad contradictions of the world. Instead, he wanted his actors to make these contradictions visible, to show the causal link between wealth and poverty and money and power, and expose the different sides of the argument in such a way as to encourage debate. Thus in *The Caucasian Chalk Circle* he was keen to show that his working class 'heroine', Grusha, was a 'sucker' (he used the American term) in following her 'natural' maternal instincts; she would have been much better off if she had ignored the abandoned Michael. Similarly, in the same play, he wanted to make plain that instead of being a canny peasant judge with sympathies for his own class, Azdak is deeply corrupt; Brecht's point is that it is only in conditions of such corruption that the poor stand any chance of receiving justice.

These observations, and the obsessive interest in contradiction, are almost counter-intuitive and go beyond the usual notions of 'common sense' or 'nature'. But Brecht's realism is dialectical, and acting in his plays, or approaching other plays in a Brechtian way, requires 'complex seeing' above all.

Simplicity

It is for all these reasons that Brecht's theatre has a reputation for such fearsome difficulty. At its heart, however, he was involved in a search for simplicity. This is not the aesthetic purity of Peter Brook's 'empty space', nor the psychological truth of Stanislavsky's system, let alone the religiosity of Grotwoski's 'poor theatre' or Artaud's 'theatre of cruelty'. Instead Brecht's response derives from a realistic view of the world and a reaction to its injustice and despair. His last poem expresses this perfectly:

> *'And I always thought: the very simplest words*
> *Must be enough. When I say what things are like*
> *Everyone's heart must be torn to shreds.*
> *That you'll go down if you don't stand up for yourself*
> *Surely you see that.'*(6)

Summary

One of Brecht's favourite phrases was Hegel's 'the truth is concrete'. In this spirit, it is perhaps worth venturing ten points to remember when acting in a Brecht play, or using Brechtian techniques with plays by other dramatists:

1 Work out what the writer is trying to show in every moment of the play and make sure it is evident in your performance.

2 Remember your audience and seek out their involvement and participation: acting is more than mere self-gratification.

3 Look for the contradictions in your character and work out how to show them.

4 Examine your part from the point of view of its economic and social circumstances and explore the way that these factors shape your actions throughout the play.

5 Ensure that everything you do tells the story as clearly as possible and understand your character's role in the story.

6 Look at every moment of decision and work out how to show the audience the thought process involved.

7 Refrain from trying to make the audience 'love' your character and avoid sentimentality; instead, present the audience with all the complexity and multiplicity that is characteristic of the real world.

8 Recognise that the world is made up of material objects and ensure that you understand the way that these have value; the most noble visions are

dependent on the most basic human needs – food, shelter and safety – and you should ensure that your performance makes this plain.

9   Understand that acting can explain even as it entertains, provoke even as it stimulates, and let your work as an actor inform your understanding of the world.

10 Let this understanding of the world motivate your work as an actor.

Brecht After Brecht

Brecht devised his theatrical theories above all for directing, designing and acting in his own plays, but he had a lifelong interest in a vast range of other dramatists, from the Greeks and Shakespeare, through 18th and 19th Century European drama, to Maxim Gorky, Sean O'Casey and other left-wing 20th Century dramatists. A Brechtian approach to acting in their plays can be enormously fruitful.

Brecht stole many of his ideas about the theatre from Shakespeare, and acting in Shakespeare's plays benefits a great deal from a Brechtian approach – particularly an understanding of the play's political and social content. A Brechtian approach to Shakespeare would focus on the simple, gestic nature of Shakespeare's stagecraft, the epic structure of his story-telling and the clear presentation of contradiction and complexity. It would also employ an active and knowing relationship with the audience, with soliloquy and asides operating as direct commentary and learn from the original theatrical form.

Brecht joked that Shakespeare's theatre was *'full of A effects'*(7), and a version of the 'alienation effect' is very useful: when working on a production of *King Lear*, Timothy West said to me that he thought that Lear in the first scene was self-indulgent; I agreed and he played the scene with this in mind. The performance wasn't cold, it just didn't demand that the audience love Lear as soon as he came on stage. Done properly, the alienation effect is one of the key features of realistic acting in Shakespeare.

Acting in 18th Century European drama benefits from the Brechtian approach too, in that it emphasises the social and political realities that underpin the comedy, intrigue and romance. And Brecht's emphasis on story-telling is vitally important in clarifying the lines of dramatic action which can be obscured under wit, language and stylish surface. As in Shakespeare, the Brechtian relationship with the audience has many affinities with the theatrical self-consciousness of the drama of this period.

It is sometimes presumed that Stanislavski and Brecht are diametrically opposed in their views about acting. However, it is clear that Brecht had genuine respect for the great Russian director (see *Some of the Things That Can Be Learnt from Stanislavski*), even if he felt that Stanislavski's theatre was not suitable for describing the realities of 20th Century experience. Furthermore, as Peter Stein has shown, a combination of Stanislavskian attention to psychological detail with a Brechtian enquiry into social questions can be immensely rewarding. It is one of the ironies of Brecht's life that he spent a few days with Lee Strasberg, the founder of the American 'method' school of acting, working on *The Decision*. In a letter to Strasberg, Brecht wrote that they broke off their collaboration for 'political reasons': *'It is a great pity because I had the impression that we worked very well together'* (8).

The influence of Brecht can be felt in much contemporary theatre too: direct address, physical expressiveness, theatrical fragmentation and so on. What is usually missing is the depth of Brecht's political analysis and, enjoyable as such inventive work can be, it can rarely be described as 'Brechtian'.

DISCUSSION POINTS

Brecht wanted his gravestone to say: 'He made suggestions, others carried them out.' The following questions are intended to provoke discussion: they do not have a right or wrong answer.

- Brecht was concerned that his theatre should relate to the real world. So why is his theatre different from 19th Century naturalism?

- Brecht asked his audience not to deposit their brains in the cloakroom with their hats when they go to the theatre. So why are his best plays so theatrical, full of dramatic incident and rich with character and colour?

- Brecht wanted his theatre to address the issues of the modern world. So why are so many of his plays set in the past and why was he so keen on historical distancing in approaching the classics?

- Brecht stated that modern content required a modern form. So why do his plays so often draw on traditional form?

- Brecht's characters are highly contradictory. Wouldn't it have been better if he had ironed out these contradictions and made his characters more straightforward?

- Brecht's characters are the product of their economic situation and environment. Surely this leaves no room for the actor to show psychology and the inner life?

- Brecht wanted his actors to 'show what needs to be shown'. Surely this results in two-dimensional characterisation?

- Brecht believed in socialist revolution. Surely the collapse of the Soviet Union and the dominance of Western capitalism invalidates his plays?

Further Reading

Brecht's most important theoretical works are *The Messingkauf Dialogues*, published in a single volume by Methuen (1975), edited by John Willett and *A Short Organum for the Theatre* (1948, Methuen) to be found in John Willett's outstanding collection of essays, *Brecht on Theatre* (1957, Methuen). Marc Silbermann's *Brecht on Film and Radio* (2000, Methuen) and Tom Kuhn and Steve Giles' *Brecht on Art and Politics* (2004, Methuen) contain more specialist pieces.

Brecht's German is notoriously difficult to translate and some commentators feel that no one has managed to render his peculiarly allusive language satisfactorily. Brecht's first English translator was the American scholar, Eric Bentley, whose fine, if somewhat colloquial, translations were published by Grove Press. British readers are fortunate to have had John Willett, Ralph Manheim and Tom Kuhn as joint editors of Methuen's eight volumes of *Collected Plays*. Their superbly detailed editions provide the reader with the best available account. They also produced definitive volumes of the *Poems*, *Letters*, *Songs from the Plays*, *Short Stories* and *Journals*, all of which are rich with insights. The British theatre has commissioned a number of translations by contemporary writers – including David Hare, Hanif Kureishi, Howard Brenton and Steve Gooch – with varying degrees of success.

Brecht has attracted a great deal of critical commentary, of all kinds: the two most reliable studies in English are Keith Dickson's *Towards Utopia* (1978, Oxford University Press) and John Willett's *Brecht in Context* (1984, Methuen). The same author's *Theatre of Bertolt Brecht* (1977, Methuen) is invaluable, as is *The Cambridge Companion to Brecht* (1994), edited by Peter Thomson and Glendyr Sacks. My own *Guide to the Plays of Bertolt Brecht* (2006, Methuen) attempts to provide an entry level approach to the subject, suitable for students and actors alike.

One of the most important works, published in Brecht's own lifetime, is Walter Benjamin's individual essays which have been collected under the title *Understanding Brecht* (1998, Verso). The best biographies are by Frederic Ewen (1967) and Klaus Volker (1979).

Notes and References

(1) Brecht, B. – *Man Equals Man*. Methuen, 1979

(2) Brecht, B. – *The Mother and Six Lehrstücke*. Methuen, 2003

(3) Brecht, B. – *Journals 1934-1955*. Methuen, 1994

(4) Brecht, B. – *A Short Organum for the Theatre from Brecht on Theatre*. Methuen, 1957

(5) Brecht, B. – *Letters*. Methuen, 1990

(6) Brecht, B. – *Poems*. Methuen, 1987

(7) Brecht, B. – *Messingkauf Dialogues*. Methuen, 1975

(8) Brecht, B. – *Letters*. Methuen, 1990